Sophie's World

JOURNEYS OF THE LOST SOUL

SOPHIE MUBVUMBI JAYAWARDENE

Order this book online at www.sophiesworldthejourneys.com

email sophiesworldthejourneys@gmail.com

Printed in the United States of America.

ISBN: 978-1-4669-3918-9 (sc)
ISBN: 978-1-4669-3917-2 (hc)
ISBN: 978-1-4669-3919-6 (e)

Library of Congress Control Number: 2012909801

Trafford rev. 07/31/2012

 www.trafford.com

North America & international
toll-free: 1 888 232 4444 (USA & Canada)
phone: 250 383 6864 ♦ fax: 812 355 4082
email orders @trafford.com

ABOUT THE BOOK

A true story about a woman called Sophie Mubvumbi Jayawardene born in 1963 in Rhodesia now Zimbabwe. She moved to New Zealand in 1988 with her husband and her two children in search of a better life. Shortly after moving to New Zealand she was diagnosed with a killer diesease of the century. She was told she was the first to have this dieases and her case was to be refered to the govrnment authority. At the time of diagnosis Sophie was six months pregnant with twins. She learnt that she had five years to live during an official meeting. Her residence status was to be provoked if she would leave the country with the intension to come back. The authority feared her unborn babies left to come into the world would spread more dieases they ruled to abort. Under her circumstances she could not afford to go back to her country. The only option was to let them take care of her babies the way they had suggested. This was never to be mentioned again even in the dark. Lost, confussed, scared, isolated and lonely her ordeal was just starting. For many years that came Sophie straggled to understand what had happened to her. At thirty one years she separated from her husband ,alone and scared she did out lived the five year sentence. Sophie became someone else from the person she had been since she arrived in her new country. She lived a life packed with drama, tragic, abuse while walking on the darkest side. On her walks she had two little people to protect. Fourteen years after the diagnosis Sophie fell to the ground. For three years she lay on a death bed straggling to understand what happened to her. Sophie began to question the meaning of life and if she should come back to life what was the purpose of it all. Fortunately she stamble on a jigsaw pazzle that had all the answeres she required if she should be lucky enough to have a second chance. It is this time she discovered a cure a cure with conditions and the first of its kind. Sophie did not know what was to come or if all the pieces where in the pack . . . A powerful story to read.

CONTENTS

DEDICATION

*M*y story is dedicated to my family I left in Zimbabwe. My mother, brothers, sisters, many of who passed away without knowing what had happened to me. I am forever truly sorry for all that I caused.

Knowledge: I can never ask for a better son than the one you are. You are the man in my life and the father that I once grieved for. Thank you for being my son and friend, and for loving me.

Rohini: my daughter and my best friend. How could I ever be anywhere in this world without a caring being like you? You have comforted me and nurtured me beyond anyone should expect a child to take on. You have been the mother to all of us. You have always said, "You don't have another daughter, Mamma." Yes, my darling daughter, I have only one daughter to love and cherish.

Kingston Jayantha Farai Jayawardene Hassleburg—my grandson, my mate, and my dream little man.

Rohan: my best friend, father, and granddad to my children. My father said, "Regardless of what will happen, Rohan is an honorary man." I said, "What does honorary mean?" He replied, "A good man." He could not have been wrong. You were the brother in my past life, and I will always love and cherish our co-existence.

ACKNOWLEDGMENTS

This space is dividable
Is dividable into millions and millions of names
Every path I have walked and yet to walk
I have passed by you
I have smiled at you
I have laughed with you
I have screamed at you
I have cried with you
I have cried for you
I have wished for you
I have hoped for you
I have been angry with you
I have been pleased with you
I have eaten with you
I have dreamed about you
I have learnt from you
I have thought of you
I have missed you
This place is dividable into millions of names

You are the shadow
The shadow of my bones
The shadow of my soul
The shadow of my spirit
The shadow of my being
This space is dividable into millions of names

You are the leaves in my river
The twigs in my river
The log in my river

The fish in my river
The crocodile in my river
The hippo in my river
The reed in my river
The alien in my river
This space is dividable into millions of names

You are the water
The water in my path
This space is dividable into million and million of names

Special Thanks

Rohini Jayawardene. You know why I can't say what I am thankful for. Love you with all my heart.

Thank you, Dr. M. Pohl, for being my GP and THEE . . . GP.

Thank you, Dr. Pegler, former head of the Infectious Disease Ward, Auckland Hospital, and the staff of Ward Nine, 2001 to 2005.

In Australia, thank you to the Gay couple that looked after me in 1989. Sorry I never had the chance to thank you.

I am thankful to the other hospital doctors and the staff that made all the difference in my life. You all allowed me to witness the work nurses and doctors do to save lives. To all the medical staff around the world, thank you for your undivided attention and your hearts of gold. Your profession is deeply and forever highly regarded in my opinion.

Mr. Oliver, for being a friend, for helping me to overcome the shame and fear, for giving me the courage. For offering a hand to my family wherever I could not manage. Thank you.

Pioneer Finance NZ. Thank you for lending me the resource for the last piece of the jigsaw puzzle I so needed to participate in this world.

Footsteps of a Dream

*F*ourteen years later, I found myself thinking, "Now everything makes sense." I could see and breathe again. The jungle had disappeared and the world reappeared. The impossible had become possible; in a blink of the eye, the search for the lost ship was called off. "How on earth did all this happen?" I whispered almost as if I had company.

Like a dream on a rainy Sunday afternoon nap, I received a sign, a sign that I had longed for, a sign that triggered my mother's words: "What conceals what is inside a home is the roof." These words were a tool in motivating me to stay in shape. Keeping in shape was not what my mother had meant; she meant how to avoid being a laughing stock. She had spoken of how someone's misfortunes entertained another. On one of my favorite television shows called *Keeping up Appearances*, I had laughed through the one-hour episode as this show had some elements of what my mother meant. Keeping in shape had been always a tool that served multiple purposes and been a must for the purpose of disguising what is inside my body.

On this particular evening I was going through my normal routine of yoga mixed with other exercise movements created way before the gym technology. I exercised once a day after dinner in my living room. At this stage I exercised only because I was thinking if I didn't, my body would seize. I was no longer concerned about my mother's words. I was a fragile looking frame, almost like a skeleton. At the end of my exercise, I decided to wind it up with a (calming) exercise method that I had read in a yoga book some years earlier. I had tried this exercise and failed many a times. To focus on one thing was like inviting an alien to a scientist's inventions day. I had a thousand things coming in and out of my brain like a motorway in a modern city. Only God knew how one got out through which exit.

Back to my routine, I lay down on my stomach, shut my eyes, and created a place where it felt peaceful and comforting as the yoga book had said. Something must have changed for me to consider attempting this exercise without muttering, "There is no place I find peaceful," a thought that was always on my mind. I closed my eyes to imagine this vision. I visualized a park in which there was a lake on a hot bright blue sky day. Some huge tree with small leaves that resembled those of silver fern plant stood heavily around the park. The trees were beatified by purple flowers and stood still as there was no wind. For the most part, the scent of the flowers had a strong masculine fragrance. As I lay under the tree indulging in the fragrance of the flowers, I feel asleep.

This routine is not supposed to take more than five minutes; instead, I lay there and woke up only an hour later. While sleeping, I experienced total peace, though in my sleep I knew I had met a person who was me. Strange enough I had experienced what peace was momentarily. "I can find a place where there is peace. No! I have found peace!" I screamed with joy as I woke up. "Why a Jacaranda Park?" I questioned as I recalled the familiarity of the trees in my imagination. I could still smell the scent of the trees; it was that of a Jacaranda tree. The calming environment I had created in my imagination was not just an imagination—I had been to a place like this before. Immediately my heart sank.

Like a zooming lens of a camera, my brains zoomed a millions miles, over the ocean, to a place I had intended to forget. On remembering that this place was once my homeland, the familiar hot tears poured down my cheeks. I sobered quietly as if there was someone nearby, of whom I did not want to hear me crying. I went back to sleep still on the mat I had been exercising on. Only this time I slept till the next morning.

When I was young, I had the opportunity to leave the village I was born in. My mum had taken my brothers and me during school holidays to visit Dad. Dad worked in Salisbury which was the capital of Rhodesia. There I had seen very huge trees alongside most roads, especially Manukau Road, the one that led us into the city. I had then associated Jacaranda trees as a symbol of my city. I did recall how beautiful they were and the captivating scent that lingered in the air. When the Jacaranda trees shed their flowers, the flowers would create lawns and streets of exuberant purple. It was magnificent to look at. Every time I was in the city, this picture postcard scene was the only sophisticated place I had seen.

Later in life, my first home was in a suburb that used to belong to whites only. I liked whites-only suburbs as they had beautiful houses on huge sections. Nearly every house had a tennis court and a swimming pool. Somehow the Jacaranda trees stood not far from every home. My house was on an intersection, and both sides of these roads had huge Jacaranda trees. I never did consciously adore nature, even the huge trees that clearly looked like a landmark. I swear if anyone before this day had asked me to name one tree, Jacaranda was never one name I would come up with.

"The Jacaranda tree, an awakening omen, Or was it a sign of who I am!" In a split of time I became aware that my past was creeping on me. The coldest chill ran through my body and I gasped. My past was creeping back to me like an African kitchen lizard. I felt empowered, fascinated, and a wave of fright ran through my body. Another of my journeys was just beginning, or the one I was traveling on was continuing. Either way this time I was not sure what sort of methods of traveling will be put in place.

My mind in the same instance rushed to the methods of traveling I had endured in the past. I had traveled intensively in my dreams from a very young age. I dreamt in my sleep more than a fortune-teller would for purposes of work. I dreamed so much that after years of dreaming the dreams suddenly stopped. I had not dreamed or given a thought for many years to this day. I had tried blocking the memories, except the effects of them never leave. I had carried a feeling that was frightening, a fright that had been inflicted on me in every dream. Instead the feeling never left. The feeling had been a physical weight I dragged everywhere I went which frightened me deep inside. I was aware that I was the only one who knew of its existence. The clearness of these dreams was surely made to be remembered. On noticing that the dreams had stopped, I assumed that it was because I had left town. I was very wrong not from where I had been since I left town. Back where I had come from, I could see clearly the dreams did not vanish. They had turned into a physical form, invisible of cause but in a position where they could hold my hand and walk me through. Amazingly, the path I had walked to this day of discovery had not been any different from that I had seen in the dreams. "How cruel," I had thought. How can anything walk someone in such a scary path?

I began to experience unsettling dreams when I was twelve and told my mother. "Weird," my mother had said once. I had been telling her of my nightmares as I had thought. "They scare me, Mum, during the day as well." I had told her. Several dreams down the track and the dreams seemed to be getting weirder each time I told her. "I don't know where you are getting those dreams from?" she had said with an attitude that suggested my complaints were starting to scare her. Another time she had suggested not to sleep facing the east as this would cause nightmares. She had told me this theory because in my culture, that was a person's final resting position when being buried. I followed my mother's advice; even so the dreams did not stop. The plot of these dreams did not change; instead, they had gone darker, gone far and too scary to repeat.

However, in some dreams I had dreamt that I had wings and that I was flying above the ocean. Could it be that I had learnt to wish for wings while dreaming so I could get away. It is what was happening to me in the dreams that required an extraordinary escape. In other dreams I would find myself caught in a war zone, and I was again able to escape by flying away to a world I had not seen before. When I had tried to describe the places I was seeing in the dreams, I could find no words to describe the landscape as there were no such scenes that I had seen prior to dreaming of which I could compare with. Most of these landscape I had seen them from above; a few times I had landed far away from where the dream had started. In real life my mother had only heard of the ocean through my father or the Bible. I did not understand when she had made a remark that suggested I was a black sheep of the family.

I had dreamt of one dream that was very scary and unforgettable and never dreamt of it again. I was in a dream set on a primitive type journey, the Stone Age. It was a flat hot land covered with dense bush, a world where the vibe was dangerous and scary. In this dream this was the world I lived in. I had been walking alone through a narrow red dusty earth path. Where I was going was never in the dream. It was very quiet, except for the sound of the grass rubbing my feet. The path appeared to have been formed by different animals over a long period of time. The weather was a perfect African hot day except the feeling of the hounted havens that sat heavly above my head watching me.

As I walked for some time through the bushes, I could hear the rulers of the jungle roaring in the distance. The sound was more of growling at each other. When I had reached a distance where I could not see where I had come from or signs of any creature, there was only the vibe of danger ahead. Suddenly there were dead people with no bodies alongside the path. It appeared as if someone had taken time to display them. I walked stiffly trying not to look at the faces through the narrow path. I continued to walk steadily surrounded by these bodiless heads. Trees and shrubs were on each side as larger taller trees appeared ahead of me. The lions with their powerful voices undoubtedly held the jungle for ransom. I could hear them growling; they were perhaps keeping intruders know they were nearby. I felt I was the only moving creature left. My little bare feet managed to get me to the end of the scary part of the jungle. I had then wondered, "where were the lions?" I announced myself lucky while in the dream by saying "I must have passed this track at the right time." End of the dream. Most dreams were about animals normally in their furious moods; some dreams were about wars and I was always the hunted one.

Even then, I was surely guided by someone. I had always felt the strangeness of my dreams as if they appeared yesterday. One thing I did not know was that the dreams where I had wings and was flying over the ocean were going to be a real adventure someday. Up in the sky over the ocean I was scared, but at that stage in life, I had done OK, I had thought. I had reached maturity unnoticeable and childhood seemed like a very long time ago. I had had a home, was someone's wife and a mother. All that I was looking forward to in life was to grow together with my children and to get old.

I was just a girl from Africa who believed if you can survive in Africa no place on earth can scare you. It could have been nice if my story had an ending like, "Coming to American" dream stories that had been told around the world. Unfortunately or fortunately, my trip from Africa wasn't taking me to America. Those many years ago America and Britain were the only places called "abroad" by many Africans. Most of those people who traveled were fortunate and this "going abroad" thing was not a conscious decision to many black children. Some people were awarded scholarships by missionaries; either way it was a ticket to a better world. In my growing up days I was never exposed to a society that traveled abroad or even daydreamed of the concept. When my husband had suggested he was taking the kids and me to the Western world, I was excited and also frightened.

The day we left, my family came to see the kids, and we took off. The 707 airplane we were to travel in, stood like a big bird on the runway. A little fright ran through my heart at the sight of it but had no time to be scared. I was already filled with emotions of leaving my family behind. For a moment I forgot about what I was feeling. I had never seen the inside of a plane. As I boarded the plane, I was captured by the rich smell of the leather interiors and pretty, white air hostesses whose dress and manners were that of the West. The aeroplane engine started and that was nothing I had thought it would be like. My whole world collapsed. Tears were already running hot, and there was no turning back. I kept walking toward my seat I had been instructed to take, holding the tears back. In the plane I sat between my children—Knowledge, aged six, and Rohini, three and half. I realize that my kids and I were the only black people in the plane.

In any other situation I could have been scared. Then, how many black people were as fortunate as me, I thought momentarily.

I managed to listen to the voice that said, "I am your Captain," and soon an air hostess took over with the safety instruction: "In an emergency situation make sure you put your jacket first before you attend to someone." I ignored those words; I did not want to think of the situation that will be awaiting on the ground if that should occur. I knew for most of my journey I would be traveling above the ocean. The engine grew louder and louder, and off we were in the air. I cried myself to sleep and only woke up when the hostess had asked if we would like some dinner.

I looked up where the gentle friendly voice was coming from, then sideways. I was greeted by two sets of eyes that looked excited about having dinner. I looked at the pretty air hostess who was standing next to me and said, "Yes please." I looked around for the second time to check if by any chance there might be some black people sitting at the back. This time I failed to create any fear that related to being the only different person. I was not the only different person after all—there was my children right next to me. I could still feel a huge lump of grief. I knew I had lost the world I knew. The air hostess returned with our meals and drinks. After dinner we slept all the way to Sydney. We arrived at Sydney airport at midnight where my husband had instructed me to stay the night. I piled my hand language next to a three-seater bench and put my kids to sleep. The airport was well lit and workers were carrying on with their work. It was a short sleep before travelers began to fill up the place again.

We resumed our journey first thing that morning. I had no idea how long it was going to take; it just appeared as though I was going to the end of the world—I still had one more flight to catch. My destination was Gisborne, a small town on the East Coast of the North Island of New Zealand. After what I had thought as a much shorter flight than I had experienced, we caught another flight from Auckland to Gisborne. Although this was the shortest distance we had to travel, it appeared to be a lifetime.

As we approached Gisborne, the small plane appeared to be dropping in the sea. Looking down the landscape was so scary, yet I had flown over them in my dreams. I panicked a little as time seemed to prolong for whatever reason. I was feeling as if the plane was heading straight into the sea. I did not know what to say and could not scream. I tried to concentrate on the voice of the pilot who was informing us about the weather condition. I waited for him to say, "Put on your safety gear," but nothing of the sort. I calmed myself down by holding on to both my children's hands, who were clearly enjoying the ride.

During the many hours I was changing plane to plane, country to country, and city to city, I hadn't thought of where I was going. I barely registered the transfers and the stopovers. I just wanted to get to wherever it was we were going. I finally saw a small airport by the beach. As we landed I noticed my husband and one other person waiting to welcome us.

This was the beginning of a dream, very scary yet exciting; I had never been in a plane, let alone, see the ocean that close. In my head I heard a voice of acknowledgment that said, "I had done only what other people like my mom see on television if we land safely," and we did.

Relieved to see my husband waiting at the small airport I knew I was at the end of my journey. "This is no big city," he had told me in a letter. Looking through the window of the station wagon we were traveling in to our new home, I was anxious to explore this new environment. The long flight from Zimbabwe, Sydney, Auckland, then Gisborne had not taken its toll yet; I wanted to see everything. The trip to our new home from the airport was less than ten minutes. All the way home my eyes were glued to the window of the car that was being driven by my husband's workmate. To my surprise I discovered we had passed through the city center; my husband had answered upon me asking. "Well, I must have blinked," I thought. On arrival, I found my husband had done all that was necessary to the house as he was waiting for the kids and me. The house was provided by the Ministry of Education opposite the school he was now teaching.

As days and weeks went by, I had learnt a lot regarding the education system and also the two groups of people that belonged here. I could have called them tribes back where I had come from. As my husband had explained in his letters they, were Maori people and the white people. At one stage there was an event hosting the Governor General when he was visiting. We were invited to this special event. My family and I got to see and learn a little about their culture. The most enjoyable happenings of the event were the traditional dance and their traditional foods. The culture I witnessed had very similar traits to the one I had been brought up with. Every now and then a sense of sadness sank in.

It was the month of June when we arrived in Gisborne, and boy, it was cold. My husband may have forgotten were we were coming from to arrange our arrival in such a cold season. I was in misery, especially when I had to wash clothes that never dried. It would take days at a time to dry them inside the small detached garage. It would rain for days non-stop, and this would reduce me to tears. For someone who had believed you only cried when someone died, I realized I was now crying for the smallest things, such as when I needed to go to the dairy to buy milk, I would wish I had a sister to look after my children at home in case I had a car crash. I wished I had a nanny to help me pick up the toys, make the kids beds, and babysit so we could have a night out. I wished I had a gardener so I would not have to learn to mow the lawns. Someone had asked if I was feeling homesick. I responded by asking, "What is homesick?" I was not kidding. I had not heard of this word before. "Homesick," I had noted.

The Matenga family helped this misery seize a bit. One morning a truck had stopped outside our door. A strong man walked out to my front door. It was early morning; my husband and kids had just gone to school. I stood on the doorway to talk to him. He introduced himself as Tunis Matenga. After inquiring on where I had come from, he offer on behalf of himself and his wife Magarrete to host us at his house on the coming Saturday. "Please come to my house at seven for breakfast. I will pick you and family up," he insisted.

Saturday morning we wore warm clothes and left with him. He took us straight to the Kaiti Hill. He showed us around Gisborne first, then Kaiti Hill. Kaiti Hill is by the sea not far from the wharf and there was a marae. A marae is a meeting house for Maoris where most traditional events take place such as funerals. The totem pole that stood in front of the building said a lot. "We call this a marae. Each tribe has their own and each totem pole tells a story," he had explained. As we stroll by the Kaiti beach, my kids were picking up pipis. I had no idea what that was, but it was certainly an adventure to them. We took some of the pipis with us. As we continued with the tour, we were also sharing similarities in our cultures. On telling us what Matenga means, in Maori Matenga his name means heavens. In Shona, my native language, "Matenga" with a slight different sound means heaven, also spelt the same way. We passed through the wharf were there were fisherman selling live mussels. Mr. Matenga opened one and ate it, then another and another. Apone knowing what that was, I was horrified. I have never heard of anyone eating live anything. "These men had just come from the sea and this is a fish market," he had said. I thought, "Wow, he is brave." Yes, in his appearance he was a very strong man. He later bought what he required and drove us back to meet Magarette his wife and their boys. I think they had five boys, all of them much older than my kids, and the youngest was about eight. The Matengas I assumed had strong links to their Maori roots.

Magarette had prepared a huge breakfast waiting on the table. Mr. Matenga after introducing us to his wife went and steam the muscle and pips he placed them on the table. After that day, every Saturday they had taken the kids to play rugby. News of some black family living in town circled, thanks to the local newspaper we were soon in the newspaper. Everyone wanted to see us in flesh. At the supermarket, we had been treated like stars with a difference. We had people touching our skin, hair, even make us talk so they can see if we could talk.

As time had gone by, we had met other families through the school my son was attending. Or though the best ever breakfast was the one I had at

Matenga's home. I was yet to learn a lot of dishes mostly during the week. I had been picked by other friends once a week to a coffee shop that was part of Famer's Department Store on the top floor. Pavlovas, carrot cakes, kina, hang, and a lot more Kiwi dishes were being brought to my doorstep by strangers. I was feeling at home with all this generosity from strangers. Occupied with the new way of living I soon forget about the cold weather, and time had moved.

Gisborne had the other side that was so enjoyable it's difficult to forget. When summer approached it was a place I truly enjoyed, the bright skies with all its warmth. It was charming when the sun came out. It was now summer. Believe me, after a horrible winter, I could not help myself indulging in this atmosphere. When I had learned that Gisborne was the first city in the world to see the sun, I said, "Yes! I am truly one of the lucky ones." I had not heard of a place on earth that was privileged to see the sun first. One day I woke up early morning to catch the sunrise by the beach, and the feeling was incomparable. While at the beach, I leant forward, scooped water with my palm, and took a mouthful. I quickly spit it out. My husband noticed that and gave his usual loving smile. It was his way of acceptance of who I was as such situations had happened many times since I met him. I had a lot to learn from what he knew. I did not know sea water was salty. I continued with my ritual this time liking the water and making sure it reaches my guts. "A different world indeed," I thought.

I was overwhelmed by this new discovery and remembered what my grandmother once said in an adult conversation, "A remedy for preventing catching local diseases is to take a little earth, put it in a glass of water, and drink it." As I was much younger, I do not think she thought for a moment I was listening or would ever remember this. I did spare the kids from drinking salty water as they had already been swimming in sea water. I assumed at some stage they would swallow the mighty sea water.

Everywhere I looked seemed to have the slogan "new," so I had a lot of new things to plan. Having my kids running up and down helped me with most things that I was to plan for. I could not have imagined where to start if I was there alone. Everything felt rather frightful but right and wonderful. I planned to study a year later when my youngest child had turned five. A year did rush through like floodwater. For the first Christmas, we left for Australia to visit my husband's family in Melbourne. We spent a few weeks there. When we returned, I enrolled in a computer introduction course, a government initiated program. After three months, I had my first certificate of achievement. I felt confident in what the future could bring for me and went on taking the next level. I took up business and computer studies. Life had just begun. I was shining with life and the future looked brighter than the sun. One day I would go back home and bring a niece or nephew to help them to better education, I had thought. I am the first person in my family's history to migrate overseas.

We had settled well in our new hometown. We were planning holidaying and sight seeing around New Zealand, our new country. We had made friends through schools and sports organizations alike. I had become confident enough to taking part in my children's activities, one of which was scouts groups. I was being asked to share the experience of where we had come from, as most of these kids had not seen black people. Sometime I felt like my kids were an educational tool for these isolated communities. These early days were very much a learning curve for me and felt privileged to be placed in a newspaper as the first black family to settle in Giborne, if not the first black family to set foot there. Nevertheless, I was still looking at the world the way it had been presented to me when I was growing up. I had yet to learn and understand the reason most of these kids had not left town or exposed to the world around them. All this was great for writing letters to my people, sometimes the purpose was to remind them to cherish and be happy with what they have. "The way things were here weren't the same as they watched on television," I had written in my letters.

It had been six months since the doctor had confirmed an additional member on the way. I had glowed from the doctor's clinic all the way home.

With this news, we moved from the small government provided house into a larger and private-owned home. It was then that my newly found, intriguing, and beautiful world turned grey, harsh, and cruel.

It could have been a normal day where I do normal chores. In actual fact it was a normal day despite a call I got from my GP in early May 1989. It was a beautiful sunny day, the beginning of my second winter in this town. I was not looking forward to go through another four months of misery, but by now I had a life to live. I had an appreciating attitude and was enjoying all things this town had to offer. Usually after the kids had gone to school I would clean up and spend most afternoons reading *Mills and Boon* books. It was then that my phone rang, "Is your husband home?" That was my GP on the other side.

"No," I answered politely.

"It's actually for your results. You are positive."

I had been waiting to hear from him as two weeks earlier I had visited him. I had visited him to discuss a problem that happened when I was pregnant. Previously I had been told it was blood pressure. "I am not worried, it has happened with the other pregnancies." I had told my doctor. He had suggested carrying out a blood test and referred me to Dr. Shelly Robertson a gynecologist for a checkup. With that I went home and basically carried on with my life.

I did not ask any further questions and so my GP did not elaborate on the findings. I thanked my GP and hung up. The day went on as usual waiting for my family to come home. I had not yet found out more of this till my husband got home that evening.

When my husband got home, I was happy to tell him that I was positive. "The doctor had called," I said. Marrying an educated man was one thing I had dreamed of when I was a teen. As I was the youngest girl of five older sisters, I got to observe all my sisters' lifestyles. Three of my sisters were married to laborers, and the other two were married to professional partners. These two sisters were my idols, whenever I had thought about marriage and the life I had wanted for my children. I wouldn't have gone wrong by marrying an ex-Oxford student with a degree in science, math, and had masters in engineering. When he had asked me what was positive, I replied, "I don't know." He probably knew I did not understand the word anyway, so he picked up the phone.

After he had spoken to the doctor, I would never forget the look on his face. He looked as if someone had drained all his blood. "Sophie," that's how he began, "sit down." I sat on a sofa opposite him. "Have you heard of the killer disease that makes you skinny and have dahlia bleed and die?" This is how in those days AIDS was described. I had seen a little of this once or twice on the news. People were still talking about its origin. It was mainly gay men and African people, those who eat monkeys. It took a while for me to absorb what was actually being said. As primitive as I was, I asked my husband what all that meant for me. How I had asked him that question after the description of the disease, only God knows. My husband had practiced nursing in his university years, so he had a clear understanding of what was about to happen. "The Doctor has asked us to go to his clinic tomorrow morning. Don't worry," he said. Don't worry on which part. His face and body resembles that of a person in despair and a face that was rather already dead.

On catching up to the seriousness of this my brain began to wonder. "How could this be according to how it was contracted? Surely there must be a mistake," I had thought. The next day the whole family was ordered to be tested. The days that followed only God knew what was in store for my family. I do not remember saying at least I am the only one in the family, thank God for that. I do not remember having had the time to stop and think. At the Doctor's, we were only told half the seriousness of it and that the government was to deal with us from then on.

"You are positive," my GP had said. This word when I think about it, see it on paper, or hear it, does play a joke on me. A joke that is not laughable. Six months earlier I had gone to see my GP when I had missed my menstrual cycle. He had done a pregnancy test, and when he reappeared, he said, "Congratulations, you are positive!" I had told my children when we go through one of those days when I am trying to make a point about education. I had said. "Some things you learn them from experience, there are people I know who have made it and never been to school. Learning aspects of life from different sources is part of life." That was not just a lecture but a philosophy that I did not say how that philosophy came about. I had discovered ignorance not through a fault of my own. However, in my own walking life I had discovered that, "Ignorance is a disease."

Few weeks earlier, our phone rang at night. It was on Easter Saturday. It was my brother on the other side; my husband had picked it up. I was already in bed as I had gotten tired by eight in the Gisborne heat. I heard my husband saying "Aaaaa." I could feel the deepest sorrow in his voice. It was a sound I had heard him make years ago when he had received a call from South Africa. He had received a call from his father's friend telling him that his father had died in a car crash. My heart began to race. "Sophie, it's Charles!" he called. And I knew it was my father. The previous night I had a dream about my father. In my dream my youngest aunt had poisoned my father, and I woke up screaming. I told my husband that dream before he had gone to work. Dreams had always scared me, especially this one. I had not dreamt at all since moving to New Zealand. After telling my husband, I dismissed it. I convinced myself that there was no need to worry. This was a country where superstitious does not exist. That changed within hours. "It wasn't just a dream my father had actually died. Back home my family are grieving, now this." I felt dizzy. I hurried to the loo to escape the two little eyes that were now looking at me. I came out to the sound of my husband asking me to come out. "Am I in another dream?" I could not find tears, and I wished it had remained a dream.

Grief was no longer a misfortune but a way of life. The sun did not come out anymore, and I had instantly forgotten who I was. I did not know what I was grieving about. When I had cried my husband had said, "Don't worry. I will book a plane ticket and you can go home for Christmas."

"If I am still alive," I had thought. I had cried so loud especially when my kids were at school. Most times I cried myself to sleep, and yet when I woke up nothing had changed. There was life kicking in my stomach. I would hold my stomach and try not to look at the movement on my dress caused by the baby's play.

Now I was forced to look at who was going to look after my children. Who was going to teach my daughter about womanhood? In my mind I tried to imagine which houses in that town, a town we knew nobody. Which door were my children going to knock for help? Which one of those doors would be willing to open? How my husband was going to cope? Sometimes I would trip over nothing blinded by my own tears. I would then take a nap.

I wished so much that my father hadn't died. Growing up as a child was one of the hardest things for girls, especially when something like a sudden death happens. Culturally, girls were kept separate from their fathers. I had no memories of cuddles or kisses from my dad. When I became a mother, I got to know my dad a little better, when he had come to visit us in the city. I had perceived my dad as a very intelligent man, judging by his travels. He had told me of other countries he had to visit as part of his work. He told me about different cultures so that I don't get confused after I had met my husband who was a Srilankan. The only intense conversation I ever had with my father was when I had informed him of our plans to move overseas. He had looked worried. I said, "Father, it's for the kids to get a better education."

"Don't forget us please," he seriously replied almost as if he knew something I did not know. He repeated these words again on the day of my departure.

Another thing I was not to forget was his hug at the airport, the first and last hug ever.

I was still waiting for the rain to come again, although I knew the rain was going to be very heavy this time. I also knew I was the one going to drawn. I had not known yet what the authorities were going to do. Each day seemed to have a million hours. I think somehow my children could feel that tension. I could feel the thunder, the storm, and the horrors that were to come. For the first time the role of a mother began to haunt me. In my absence, what were my children going to do and that created the beginning of panic attacks. Then I did not know what that was; just a sad heart, I believed.

If nature could bring warning signals for danger, it could have made all the difference. I was to spend most of my days daydreaming. Maybe I could have changed the nature of my pain. For many nights I lay in my bed and stared at the ceiling, crunching at my heart afraid it might jump out. I learnt to paint my face in seconds and get away from the mirror before I could see the other person that was starting to emerge.

It took a week or so for the doctor to arrange a meeting for us with the hospital officials. A meeting was to take place at Gisborne Hospital, we were told. Gisborne Hospital was less than five minutes drive from the house we lived. It had been a while since I had spoken or looked at my husband and it was no different that day. We drove up narrow roads that led to the reception. At the reception we were shown to a small isolated building, and there was a room with just about eight chairs in it. I remember this because where my husband and I were going to sit was made that obvious. A group of people in their late forties to early mid-fifties walked in. One of these people was my gynecologist Dr. Shelly Robertson. Do not imagine how I felt at this stage. I can only say it's worse than entering a courthouse for a murder sentencing. The grip on my hand of my husband seemed to tell me "I am here" although I knew his feeling too was one that of hopelessness. I was lucky to have him. Skip the introduction, I was not paying attention. I wanted to know what was going to happen to us.

"You know you have AIDS." My gynecologist had started. "This is a very serious illness. In actual fact you are the first case we have had in this country." I had a little chill in my body. I thought, "How dare I came here and introduced this disease? How did I have it?" There was no time to think about that, not now anyway. I channeled my attention back to the speaker. "There are also no drugs for this virus. Once you get it you die." She continued, "What complicates your situation is you are pregnant and that means you have passed the virus to your child." I was hoping somehow she wouldn't say those words. My pregnancy, my baby, a subject I had tried not to think about if I should not be the one to decide. My heart began to pound rapidly. I was afraid everyone in the room could see it. If I was not scared I could have said, "Excuse me, I need fresh air," but my husband's hand that rested on my lap gave me the support to remain seated. I had answered how little I knew of the disease when asked if I understood. Given the opportunity to ask any questions, I could only say, "So what's going to happen to my baby?"

Over the last few weeks I had thought about this. What I had settled for was totally about to be disregarded. I had prepared to have my baby in three months, nurture my child with miracles, and the baby was going to be fine. If anything, at least I was going to be with my baby. That I was sure of, until one of the doctors replied, "No midwife or doctor will deliver your baby. There is a lot of blood during birth and no one will take such a risk. The only way is to terminate the pregnancy and that will give you a chance to live longer." Somehow my baby could hear this. My stomach began to kick rapidly as if he was saying, "You don't have to take that option, Mum." My husband asked what about going to give birth in a different country? The only words he could manage to breathe out. As they had already contacted the so-called appropriate authorities, immigration being one of them, they had apparently already stated where they stood in relation to this case. They were not going to let us back into the country, we were told.

Not knowing what was to come, we sat there like we had been caught trying to sneak into the country. More was still to be said. "There is still a problem in New Zealand. We don't terminate pregnancy over three months," the speaker continued. In that instance we were told of their plan to solve the baby problem. We were told of a clinic called Potts Point Clinic in Sydney that specializes in abortions. "We have realized that money could be a factor in delaying doing so. Therefore, the AIDS Foundation has organized your fares and accommodation. Someone from the AIDS Foundation will get in touch with you. Meanwhile you are not to have sex with your husband. Use condoms if this is to happen." These were there last words to me and I have never seen these people again.

As the arrangements had already been made prior to the meeting at Gisborne Hospital, that evening I got a call from a lady called Judith Ackroyd, an AIDS Foundation worker letting me know she will be waiting for me at Auckland Airport. Judith was to be the person I had to contact if I should need anything regarding my condition. I met Judith the next day at Auckland Airport. When I met her she came across to me as a warm woman with empathy in her. She definitely made my journey easier. She had explained to me how my trip was going to be. I was not going to be alone in a way. She handed me with the tickets and the names of those who were to meet me at the airport. I boarded my flight as if I was a normal person even though I was aware of the aura that hung around me.

I left for Sydney where the termination was to take place. Every time I have tried to recall the emotional events of the day I left, there is a blackout. I may have said to the kids, "Mum is going shopping and your dad will look after you." I know that that day I could not have thought of how my husband was going to cope because I had been occupied with the thought since the day I found out I was going to die. I had no choice and he had no choice. I want to remember this particular day. I want to remember that morning from Gisborne Airport to Auckland, but I cannot. The only thing I do remember feeling was being a zombie rather than nervous or sad. There are many dark moments I had lived. Some are probably darker than that particular day. Only God knew the reason why that day should not be remembered. In my upbringing, an abortion was never spoken of, and I had not known that it was used as a solution to problem solving. Eating was not an option that day. I had been instructed not to eat, Judith had told me. I was not hungry. Where I was going and the reason for my travel had been all blocked. had said this once after she had come back from a funeral. Apparently, mourners had noticed a shadow where the body lay. My grandmother had told us that those who do not find their ways to heaven are the ones that hung around. The shadow we see hanging around us is the spirit that leaves when we die. Scary stuff, I had thought, not dead yet and already I knew part of me had already left. All the way to Sydney that was one thing I felt, that my spirit had left me. I felt like a shell but that feeling did not induce any need to cry.

At Sydney Airport I spotted a man holding a sign with my name. He drove me straight to the clinic. We got to the clinic quite early and checked in. This place was quiet and did not represent a slaughtering place but a business among other businesses. After notifying the clinic, the host took me to visit some place where it looked like a gay hangout. There were only males, and I was the only woman and pregnant. There was so much love in this place; most of them were couples. To my astonishment they were just cuddling or some kind of affectionate. I did not understand why my host took me there. I hadn't guessed who my host was. Nevertheless, it turned out to be a moment of peace. I did forget what I was waiting for. On our way back we passed through another place, which in memory I recognized years later as perhaps the AIDS/Gay Resource Center. The people here were friendly and sympathizing I felt.

Back to Potts Point the abortion clinic there were hundreds of women. That's what it looked like to me. I had been expecting to be the only one. When it was my turn, a short, bold, and fat doctor that looked like the olden day butcher man called my name. I walked to the reception and he handed me a green robe, then instructed me to go and have a blood test pointing to a room. Shortly after the blood test was done, he examined me and told me to go back to the waiting bay.

During this time my baby was kicking nonstop or was he just playing? I was too huge for a six months pregnant woman. I had noticed that when everyone was looking at me. I tried not to think; actually that's what I did. I was just waiting. I had been alone at some stage in life, scared, and thinking what I should be doing. This was not the kind of loneliness I had experienced. The only way I can describe the moment is this: it was like being in a small dingy room in the middle of a very still ocean. No one could see me, no one could hear me, and the only sound was that of the ocean breathing very heavily. What could I have done? Crying is supposed to be an emotional thing, I had none. The only motion I could do was shut down. At the second call I was taken to a room. In this room was a strange machine and a hospital type bed. A mask was put on my nose and out I went to sleep.

I was woken up by a bump on a stretcher bed I had been put to rest after the operation. A plumb nurse had tripped on to the bed as she spoke to the other skinny nurse. "She had twins this girl" she said it in a voice that suggested I knew how many babies I was carrying. Without much talking about their work they wheeled me out of the room. Noticing that I was already awake, they instructed me to dress while asking if I could walk. I staggered to the toilet where I felt a strange pain that summarized what the nurse had actually spoken of, "She had two babies this girl." It's over now, it's done. I came to realize of what had actually taken place. I felt empty and inhuman. "If she only knew the doctors gave up on the babies and me the minute they discover I had the virus," I had thought sadly. As usual I could take anything as if it happened to everyone all the time. This was no matter to be sorted out. It was done. Or should I have asked her what she said, or their gender? Could that have made any difference?

The nurse wheeled me out and my host was waiting with a man that he introduced to me as his partner. For a moment I ignored the pain that lingered around waiting for a slight move. I silently thought now I knew who my host was. The couple wheeled me out of the clinic to their waiting car. It was around rush hour when they were driving to their home. In the car I had been thinking of the time I had heard of the word gay. It was not long ago. Now I have met a couple and a couple that lived together. Nice one I had thought. They took me to their place which was not very far from this place. During this time I enjoyed the ride forgetting why I was there.

They had a beautiful apartment that had a feeling of love. The apartment was filled with sculptures from different countries displayed in the open covered living space. Fish ponds were neatly built in a way that resembled a fish garden, and big live plants stood in various corners offering their pleasant fresh scent. Besides being in pain I found myself admiring their lovely place, especially the largest fish that looked pregnant. While admiring the place, one of them was making me a cup of tea. They cooked dinner for me, provided bathing facilities, and even run the bath. Each time I visited the bathroom they would say, "Just leave the pads in the bathroom there, love." For a change, someone was being sensitive about another human being. Did they even know that in my culture we didn't let men see our sanitary pads let alone touching them? In my silent thought I was thankful they did not. Somewhere in the back of my mind I thought of the dangers of evening attending to my waste. Something said to me they choose to be in this situation. Someone had to do this. I dismissed that thought and enjoyed the sincere hospitality I was being provided with.

The couch I was lying on was going to be my bed for the night. That night despite the pain I felt I slept like a baby. I had learnt something new, strange maybe, but reality of change it was indeed. With that a new faith was stored in me. These two strangers had touched my hand as they spoke to me, "Good night, Sophie. If you want anything, we are upstairs." It makes sense why I did not even think about that afternoon's nightmare, not even a tear drop.

The next day they took me shopping. They had asked me if I wanted to buy anything for the kids as I could not wait to rest another day. My flight was that afternoon. I requested if they could take me to Kmart department store. I was familiar with their clothes range for kids. A couple of months before that day, I had been in Melbourne on holiday. We took the kids to Kmart and liked their range of clothes. So how could I forget the trip to Australia six months to that day? I had been married for a couple of years and had not met my in-laws who live in Melbourne. My husband did not talk much about his family prior to us visiting them for the first time.

There was something unusual when it came to the relationship between my husband and his family, but had not given a thought to what that might mean. Every child's birthday or Christmas season I never received a card from their Australian families. So I thought, they may need to meet them first. Phone calls and Christmas cards were all singled out to their beloved brother, son, and my husband. Somehow I had a feeling what that could mean also. Nevertheless, I never made it a problem until my husband announced we were to visit his family on our first Christmas abroad. After all we had moved very close to them, and we were excited at the chance of having our first Christmas away from home with our new family.

My brother-in-law picked us up from the airport, a half-an-hour trip to his house later; we were at his exclusive suburb. His brother had done well; my husband occasionally talked about his success. First impressions last; that is what we all say. In this case that's not what I encountered. When we arrived at his house, I even felt out of place for a moment without looking obvious. I am not going to describe this place but comment on its class and wealth that speaks for itself. We were shown to a room that had a couple of blankets in the corner, no beds or even a mirror. My husband was being embarrassed by this. He made the bed on the floor for four of us that evening. Strange that I am even mentioning this first encounter.

At the time I just thought, maybe they had no time to arrange for a spare bed for us.

The next day everyone went to work and my husband left to visit his mother and sister. I took the kids for a walk at a nearby shopping center. We got ourselves bits and pieces for the house. By then I wished my children were not feeling the indifference that was already starting to eat me. At dinner time my sister-in-law saved food for me and my family. I thought that was strange. I avoided talking to my husband about this as I knew he would find something positive to defuse the situation. I only hoped he remembered the way my family treated us when visiting, especially with almost a year's notice.

On the second dinner, I had the courage to ask him why we cannot eat together with his brother's family. He came up with the reason—that they were not hungry at the time they had served us dinner. How can any normal twenty-seven-year-old woman believe that? As this was a house to die for it had two dining rooms one attached to the kitchen with a living area and another dining room that I thought was for special occasions. I observed that we were being served in the kitchen/dining room. This was OK with me if this was how other cultures treated their guests, but as soon as we finished a new table for four of them immediately was made in the other dining room that I had assumed was for a special occasion. They sat and ate as if nothing was wrong, and my children had to witness this.

This was few days before Christmas. On Christmas day they were expecting a few of their friends to come for a Christmas dinner party. Surprise, surprise, we were once again served an early dinner before their guests had arrived. When their guests did arrive, being me I thought he was going to happily introduce his brother's family, especially his brother, as they hadn't seen each other for some years. That did not happen, and I sat most of the evening alone with my husband coming now and then to see if we were OK. If by this time I did not assume the reason behind the treatment, then I would have to be really dumb. After Christmas, the family took off for the New Year holiday. By then I was losing my cool—sleeping on the floor, food left on a separate fridge shelf, and above all, no one bothered to tell us they had also arranged a holiday before we came. If that was too much for me to ask then what about table talks. My in-laws could not have the decency to ask even to do with the children that they had met for the first time. I could have been better off in a motel. I don't know how I put up with such a cold environment for two weeks.

Couple of days after they had come back, my brother-in-law took us shopping at a local mall. While sitting at the back with my kids, I asked my husband if he had announced to his brother that we were going to have another baby. I had noticed that it was the end of the second week in January, and I hadn't had my last month's period. I hadn't announced this news to my husband but did so to prove a point. Maybe I was so hurt that I wanted him to understand that despite liking his family, his family had no respect for him at all. By now I was starting to understand why his family had put the distance between them and us. Marrying me or anyone else who does not come from that race is a taboo. I was thinking tough lucky, I don't really care and I did not. But I could not help recalling a conversation I had with my father before I left home. My father had told me about my husband's origins. I disputed that because I had thought I was marrying a man from Britain. He reminded me of his name and told me what he knew about his stay in England. At least my father was a clever man. I had watched him having long conversations with my husband. What I did not know was, he was asking the things I should have asked. Despite all this my father was a very educated man and had traveled intensely. Naive is probably what I was. I began to remember what my father said, "Keep your passport safe, and your return ticket in case something goes wrong. And do not leave the kids, whatever you do." So is this what he was worried about. He knew about people that do not mix, who have had the sensitivity chip removed from the day they were born.

While I was daydreaming about my father's wisdom, I was waiting for a comment from my husband or his brother. Instead I got none, except a little laugh from my husband followed by that good news some minutes later. I was furious but not because I did not get a response from him. I was thinking if he seriously thought I did not pick up that there was a problem with the way he had been behaving or did he think his brother was also that stupid? I decided I could not shop, even walk, with someone who treated other people the way this guy treated my family. I excused myself and stayed outside the mall. After a short period my brother-in-law came back. And I thought he wanted to talk, even apologize for his behavior. I find things like this funny, maybe because I have a belief too. Instead he made a comment on how my children and I were getting fat while his brother worked hard to feed us. It was like someone took a knife and stabbed me in the heart, but for some reason I felt like he hadn't taken away who I am. I unconsciously defended my pride and told my brother what I thought of him and his family and that I was not going to eat or sleep in his house for another night.

It had been over two weeks, and I had met his sister's family only once and his mother, who lived with his sister, twice. We ended up at his sister's house that evening. This time I did not want to go there. How were they going to be any different from his brother? It was getting late when we got to his sister's house. When we got out of the car, I swear I could smell more trouble; the atmosphere was cold. I assumed they were notified before our arrival. After dinner their two sons that were almost the same age as mine had been already sent to bed. His sister offered us food which I declined on behalf of myself and my kids. How cruel could I be? The kids had not eaten since lunch. Our luggage was stored in the second living room that had all the sofas covered with white sheets. In the other room sitting by the dining table were his mother, sister, sister's husband, and the brother that had brought us in. My two children and I sat on a sofa in the living room that was part of an open plan to the kitchen. Surrounded by all this was my husband who had taken a seat at the dining table.

They spoke for what appeared to be hours to each other, while we sat like refugees that had been rescued from a ship. As they were speaking in their language, I did not understand what they were talking about. It certainly wasn't about my pregnancy I had announced earlier on. The tones of their voices and body language suggested that. Above all I had to see my husband being spoken to like a school boy. Hours later when my kids had fallen asleep on my lap, we were instructed to go and sleep in the room next door, where our luggage had been stored. At least this time our sleeping room had expensive sofas and other gadgets. I saw a familiar welcome to your bedroom on the corner. A heap of blankets where piled on the floor, and it appeared one sofa had been moved to the center of the room to provide enough space. I picked up the blankets and made a bed on the floor. I was too tired, and when I woke up in the morning, my husband was not with us.

Voices in the same tone came out of the corridor, so I went to see if the discussion was still going on. I knocked on the door where the voices where coming from. What I saw in this room almost brought tears to my eyes. It was my husband sitting on one bed in the room. On the other side was his mother in another bed. Standing and talking to them was his brother-in-law. I had no idea how long their discussion went on the night before. What I knew was I was the subject, a subject that had brought shame to their family. I was positive this time that the sleeping arrangement was designed, never to let their children see a man of his culture, their beloved uncle, sleeping in the same room with black people. I politely asked my husband outside. He put on his shirt, then followed me outside. I demanded that we leave that instant. Unfortunately, we could not get a flight back to New Zealand for two more nights. For those two days, I woke up early in the morning wash the kids and take them to the mall for breakfast and lunch. In the evening, I would buy cooked dinner and share with them at the park nearby, then go back to supposedly our family. Also during these two days my mother-in-law took time to make me understand that my marriage was invalid and the children are unaccounted for in their family. That my husband's desirable bride was waiting not very far from the continent I had my foot on. I felt sorry for her not because she was old but purely someone who has never experienced falling in love.

I had only one thing occupying my mind. I was going to visit a doctor to find out if I was pregnant, not if I had suffered stress caused by the rejection I had experienced from my in-laws. I had accepted that my family is the one I left in Zimbabwe the minute I boarded the plane from Melbourne. The news of my father's death on Good Friday and the result of the doctor's visit in May had left me with the darkest sadness, fear, and regrets. "Why my father did not tell me specifics?" What am I going to do when my mother in-law bring this woman she claims to be waiting to marry my husband? What could I have shared with my father if I knew he was going to die? "Stop it, all that is not important now," I had told myself. "I am going to die. Whose side is my husband going to take, his mother's or that of his undesirable children?" I closed my eyes on that thought and quickly realized I was crossing a busy road and dismissed it.

That day, six months later, crossing a very busy road in Sydney, I suddenly thought, clothes from Kmart weren't the only thing I had brought back after that horrible holiday in Melbourne. I came back pregnant with the babies I had just given up on, the babies I could not protect. Maybe this was meant to be, and fortunately, my babies called Australia home. Even that thought was interrupted by the figure that appeared ahead of me. As we crossed that busy road, I saw my father crossing from the opposite direction. This road was busy with traffic and people. I kept walking while simultaneously looking back. I got to the other end of the road and I looked back. At the same time he did the same move. I looked again and he was gone. "There is no way my father could have crossed that road in real life at that speed. He had a stroke some ten years earlier and had died last month," I thought.

After he disappeared I immediately said to these guys, "Aay! I just saw my father." I do not think that made sense to them as the night before they had sat with me after dinner and talked about my family. They might have thought it was the anesthetic from the day before at the clinic. This part of my life makes me feel like I don't have the capacity to appreciate good people. These guys did not just give me their place to crash, they had real hearts. Wrapped in my thoughts, I never contacted this gay couple, yet I think about them all the time. And I wish one day I will be able to meet them.

After I had arrived back in Gisborne, there was a fog. Only I could see it. The weather had changed permanently to dark day and. A friend of mine and also my neighbor on seeing me the next day after my Austrlian trip noticed something. I was not pregnant anymore. As I was so fond of Rachel and her family I had already thought this moment. I think this is first time I had conciously created a lie. That wasn't hard people have miscarriages all the time. As my pregnancy was nearly due, I had to create a real lie to suit. The weather was not the only thing that was changing—there were changes in the way I felt about the locals. "Are they wondering if I am contagious or can they see through my fears?" I already was a tourist attraction in this small and isolated town; every trip out of our house we were treated like superstars in a shopping mall. Most people had never seen a black person in the flesh. I did not mind them touching our skin and feeling our fuzzy hair. All of a sudden this was no longer a good idea, of making friends. The already made friends had to be ignored and life was now moving in slow motion. The once beautiful place that I had thought it was, started whispering words in my head, "Get out of here. It's not safe and soon everyone will know who you are. Move, move, move." At the end of that year, we left the town looking for a place we could make a fresh start. We moved to an area called Bay of Plenty to a town called Edgecumbe.

We had packed our belongings and store them in Whakatane, a nearby town to Edgecumbe. My husband had promised to send me home by Christmas. I did my best to prepare for the journey home as well as preparing to come back to a new town. I am not sure why I went home because the fact that my father had passed away six months earlier did not appear to be the reason I was there. During this time I was occupied with the virus. I was not to tell my family as the rumors of the virus itself was beginning to manifest into some homes. When I had left no one had known of this virus. It felt as if everyone was for a a storm that was to end the world. Even so it was whispers in secrets and anonymously to those families that had witness its cruel takings. I could not tell my mother that Sophie is gone, and I was her stuffed up image. I knew what this would do to the family, especially my brother who had known of his school friend's death through AIDS. I got to see my family for a month but my home was no longer what I had been thinking about the time I was in Gisborne when feeling home sick. The day I boarded my plane to come back, I could feel a strong wall closing behind me, no more Mother Africa for Sophie I cried for the last time, I was no more to them, I was on my way to a new place where nobody knows my name.

Edgecumbe is in the province of Bay of Plenty. Where I went from here, what I saw and what I did was nothing like what I had prepared for. I was feeling like I was inside egg waiting to be hatched. With our life in limbo, I did not want anything hatched at all. I was feeling as if I was stuffed with some unexplainable explosives. The whole me had been ripped, shredded, and waiting to be disposed in an incinerator. Here we were back to face our fate, a fate that had not shown its true face yet.

I was lucky when my husband was good at being the head of the family. He had returned early from his Christmas break. We had settled down in the eyes of strangers. Reality was yet to begin. The only time we talked was when interacting with the kids. My husband and I knew we were faced with the unknown. We also had lost what to share as husband and wife way back in Gisborne. As a multi-cultured family, we looked different, but my family was a lot more different from what the eye could see.

Edgecumbe had a college, a primary school, a small mall, and nothing much in the way of employment. I got a night job packing oranges in orchards, the only jobs that seemed to have been available. Few weeks later being an orchard worker proved too hard for my battered emotions, and I had grown a little overweight, from dress size 10 to 18. I could not stand all night carrying heavy baskets despite the good pay. I quit after a few weeks. My husband suggested studying at a nearby polytechnic in Whakatane instead. That sounded wonderful as I had enjoyed studying the previous year. I enrolled in a business technology course part time. My husband was teaching at Edgecumbe College, teaching physics and mathematics, where he also enrolled me to study Sixth Form Certificate as an adult. I was happy doing something that would allow me to achieve higher qualifications.

We spent most of our weekends fishing by the river sanctuary and swimming at the beach. We had gone shopping some weekends to Tauranga or Rotorua, few of the nearby cities. We were spoilt for choice when it came to which town we should visit. Tauranga was just up the road so also Rotorua and Taupo, all in the heart of Bay of Plenty. At some stage, we did dismiss Rotorua as the mud smells induced vomiting in my son. The surroundings of this region had a lot more to offer. We were surrounded by rivers and lakes for fishing with bush tracks for walks. We had occasionally let the few locals we had come to know show us their unique talents, such as salmon fishing, even dear hunting.

Our house was in Matipo place, a cul-de-sac street. At the end of it was a walkway that led to Edgcumbe College and Primary School were my kids attended and their Father teaching at the college. I had two lovely neighbors. One was Mrs. Davey, who I wish to make a particular mention of. Mrs. Davey took pleasure in treating my family as hers. She was even more special because my kid's principal was Mrs. and Mr. Davey's son.

I would like to think I saw my own mother in Mrs. Davey. When I had crossed the road alone for a chat, she taught me how to bake, and she had kept an eye on the kids when they played on the road. I had known her for a short time when I heard that she had been to chemotherapy treatment the days I had not seen her. I had not heard of this before. So I was not aware how serious it was. Mrs. Davey passed away later that year. I was very sad but also happy that I got to catch the glimpse of a happily lived life. When I had looked over the fence and not seen her in her kitchen, I had felt sad. It was the good memories that would brighten my face. I had said many a times that "I want to be like her when I grew old." Sometimes I had felt sad I would open my kitchen drawer to look at the cook books she had given me. As I had never allowed myself to giving affectionate gestures in the open, I had done this by hugging the book. I had wished she had come to know the person I was in the spirit life. The only people I had started counting on were those who could not defend me here on earth. That saddened me deeply.

After the termination of my babies, my body was never the same. I had not thought of access to doctors from this place even though I was in pain most of the time. I resisted contacting any kind of medical professionals if I could help it. One occasion and the taste of what was to come is when I had put off the pain coming from the wisdom tooth. On this day my face had swollen up, and I could not take the pain anymore. My husband called Judith who arranged an appointment at Rotorua Hospital. I had not thought of how difficult it was going to be each time I needed a physician. On my appointment day I got to the hospital not knowing what to expect. The dentist who had already been informed of my condition saw me and advised that the tooth was to be removed immediately. In normal circumstances, he would have waited for the swelling to go down, since I had traveled all the way to Rotorua. It was best he removed it, he had explained. I was not scared as I had never had a tooth taken off. When he had numbed the gum and begun the procedure, it felt like he was pulling my brains out. When the tooth had come out I resumed my hour trip back to Egdecumbe.

With me were my six-year-old daughter and my nine-year-old son. The road to Egdecumbe from Rotorua is mainly forest and gorge. Half an hour later, the anesthetic ran out, and we were not even halfway back. The toothache began to accelerate. I don't think I had experienced pain like that before. I was not familiar with this road as we were new in the area. I was scared to stop. The gorge wound round and round up and down through some dense bushes, and stopping was not an option. I drove while crying. Suddenly, I heard a small voice saying, "Mamma, I know how to drive. Let me drive you home." I looked at my son who would always sit in the front seat in his father's upsences. His face was covered with tears.

I tried to answer but carried on to wipe the blood that was dripping from the corner of my mouth. He repeated those words with so much sincerity. I could not answer as I was afraid the cotton preventing the blood from spating out from the raw gap may drop. I managed to wipe my own tear and gave him a reassuring look. We managed to get home and Daddy took over the rest, and I went to sleep after a couple of Panadol. I wept as those words of braveness echoed in my head. One thing I thought that evening was, I will teach him how to drive the minute he turns eleven. I became aware that one day this will happen were I cannot say no.

Unfortunately, this was not the end of long-distance trips to the doctor. As I had been suffering from a pain in the groin that was affecting my hip movements, I got in touch with Judith Ackroyd, who referred me to Dr. Tingi, whose clinic was in Tauranga. The news was not so good. He referred me to Hamilton Hospital for a CT scan. I was informed of the diagnosis. The CT scan had found a cyst on my liver. My husband did accompany me on this day. As usual he had to explain it to me in simple details. Dr. Tingi had insisted that there was nothing to worry about.

I had been in for a CT scan twice by the end of the year keeping an eye on the cyst. The pain was not getting any better. Dr. Tingi almost became my counselor as the trips to his clinic had increased to every month, sometimes twice. It felt like I was imagining the pain especially from the history I had accumulated in my files.

"Someone or some people had gone a great deal to hide someone without concern. People had decided this was the best solution for me. But they did not ask me how I felt, nor did they show a bit of pity." I had begun to replay the events of the past two years hoping I could figure out where the pain was coming from. I had begun to wonder about what had happened in Gisborne Hospital, what they would have said in their tearoom the day the "appropriate authorities" decided my fate. I knew they talked or shared about their day's work. I was beginning to doubt if my case was even given a thought or talked about. I had assumed that someone in the tearoom could have said, "Let's get a second opinion from a higher source." If this had happened, I was imagining words like, "everyone in the health department, social development, human rights, and the immigration agrees." Or were they at the meeting I just did not listen to the introduction? "After all, the solution to the problem was pre-made for me, as if I was in capitated," I thought pitying myself. I am not sure why I was now occupied by this matter 24/7 yet I had a new dilemma to worry about.

Having diagnosed with liver cancer prompted the need for a bigger city where we could have access to better medical treatment when required. We had planned to leave Edgecumbe if I should be accepted at Auckland Teacher's Training College. I had been accepted, and it was the end of the year. It was time to go and see Doctor Ting for my last CT scan result and say a good-bye. All this time I was worrying about losing the only doctor I had grown to trust. Moving to Auckland was not an exciting adventure, just a trip to a no-man's-land. I did make an appointment to see my Tauranga doctor for the very last time.

As usual he had greeted me with sincere kindness. I was always happy to see him as I felt that he was the first doctor to call me his patient. "The test result shows the lump on your liver has not shown any growth," he said. I thought silently for a minute wondering if I should share with him what had been my theory about the lump. When I had gathered my strength not to look too investigative, I asked, "Is it possible that I may have been born like that, Doctor, since I was not born in a hospital?" As I disclose this information to my doctor, I recall the first time I met a doctor. It was when I had a stillborn child, my first baby at eighteen years of age.

My body and soul suddenly went under very high emotions; tears ran down my cheeks and I could not prevent the sobbing that followed. It had triggered the memories of the death of my first child. I got pregnant at the army camp. Very scared how I was going to tell my sister, I moved in with my friend Gladys. I had concealed the pregnancy with baggy clothes for nine months, so I had thought. Gladys was a couple of years older than me. She was more established and a mother of two. One day she went away for the weekend, and I was home alone. I felt what I thought was tummy pain. After a day and a night, I felt something pushing down my spine, and I realized that the baby was coming. I made a bed on the floor then to support my lower back with a pillow and kept my legs apart. I had seen my sister giving birth this way. l gave birth to a baby boy who did not cry. Even though I was young, the baby appeared to have been dead for more than a week or so. On observing him, his skin was whitish and peeling off; it looked as if it had been in water. I covered my baby and called the ambulance. The ambulance came and took me and my baby to the hospital. At the hospital the nurse called my sister to let her know on what had happened.

When I was thinking about this day, I realized that at least my family was there. They had said, "No secrets, Sophie." They had assured me, "No problem is just for one. We are a family and we tackle problems together." Memories like these were not welcomed in my life at this stage. A secret that my family will never know if I had my way was already under control. I had made sure I will never tell them, and when I die they will never find out. For my people to remember me as the lost one serves my dignity. I had never spoken of this time to anyone. Dr. Ting waited and handed me a tissue as the flash of memories subsided. "Why am I hurting now? I am only telling doctor what he should know about my childhood," I thought and wondered how weak I had become. Although I did not tell him the details of the first encounter with doctors, he responded as if he had read what made me so sad. "If I were you, I will go home and live a normal life," he said. It was not as easy as that, but eventually that was what I did.

Maybe I was born like that. Maybe the pain was in my head, so I will go back to Edgecumbe, pack my bags, go to Auckland, and live normal. With that in mind, my family and I moved to Auckland.

In the early nineties, Auckland was clearly behind most developed cities, but to many Kiwis it was the largest city in the world. I could not find fault with that attitude as I once thought my township I grew up in was the most sophisticated area too. Then Auckland had few modern buildings that were barely noticeable as the many historical ones were outstanding. This gave Auckland a feel of a humbled old city with rooms to offer. Most businesses did not open during weekends; only retail shops opened on Saturdays till midday. I did not know much about night life, so I could only guess that it was offering what the population then could take. The whole country had a population of three million. Spending money wasn't easy; even buying clothes was a bit of a day out. Fashion hadn't caught up with this part of the world. Many Kiwis were influenced by television and had not seen much of the outside world. It was not hard to make an assumption on this if you were Sophie. As it happened the outside world was already trickling bit by bit the time I moved to Auckland.

How big or small, beautiful or unattractive, or fast or slow Auckland was really didn't matter. The reason I had moved here was to find a no-man's-land. I was looking for a jungle with a darker coverage. There was time in life I used to talk about taking a trip to Canada or Scotland when the kids grew up. These were places my husband was going to take me one day, when we had met years ago. He had shown me photos of Canadian Festivals and many more photographs he had taken around the world. Scotland and Canada had been my favorite places, I had told him. We had stopped talking about the future garbage; we had no future, and so did our kids. I had listened carefully to my body for symptoms of death every day. As for enrolling in the Teachers Training College, I don't know what I was thinking. I had started to question my future in this city. As for teaching, who would let a person with AIDS teach their children? "Welcome to Auckland," I had thought to myself concealing that sinking feeling.

Determination is the word I should use to describe how I managed to find strength. I was so determined not to die. My children needed me and I could not think of any children in this world that needed their mother more than mine. When all this was happening no one took time to explain to me about the virus except that I was going to die. "If the doctors and the physicians can't explain what AIDS actually is, then the chances are that I might be one out of millions that is going to prove miracles," I thought daydreaming endlessly. I had to hold this fantasy so close to my heart, making it a shrine. Nevertheless, I knew the society I lived in would never want people like me next door. I was scared that in my absence, the lawmakers would not hesitate to kill my two children. I was struggling to understand how the Western people could just authorize to kill two babies without a sign of sadness. Day in, day out I had some strange lyrics to play to myself: "If I did not switch off, nothing will get done, I am the only one singing the song of death and if I let the hopelessness I am feeling show, people will think I am crazy." With that I would get up, make lunch, wash my kids, take them to school, and get on with the day.

Living normal—words of wisdom from my previous doctor—was what I was trying to do. With such courage, I tried to block the pain in my groin mentally everyday as I traveled to and fro to university. One day I could not take it. I could hardly see where the road was as I drove; I made a U-turn and went to see my doctor. I was scared as I walked into doctor Pohl's clinic. I had met him immediately after we moved to Auckland. He had invited me into his practice room. After an examination, he said, "She should be admitted to the hospital right away." He gave the required instruction to the hospital, and I was on my way to Auckland Hospital.

As I had already understood that I carried a disease that is contagious, I knew I would be treated with caution. At the hospital, a single isolated room was ready for me just as I had expected. In those days a person like me would not be left in the waiting room. I hated being known as anything really thank God those days we were coded.

A very smart looking male doctor and a lady doctor came to examine me. He said I had an infected fallopian tube and immediately arranged for treatment. He ordered that I be treated with antibiotics through intravenous as he explained to my husband that I needed hospital care for few days. Left alone in the room, I asked my husband what the doctor had actually said. After he explained, I thought, "It was all left too long. This is the pain I had for the past two years." This thought was interrupted by the fear of staying in the hospital. At that moment I felt very insignificant to this planet. "My kids," I thought as the horrors I dreaded flag their existence. I had never been apart from my children overnight since the day I went to Sydney.

I could not bear sleeping in the hospital, knowing my children were home alone. I asked for permission to be admitted as day patient. As I had been in Auckland for a few months, this looked like the test of what was to come. I pulled through that and discovered that the pain diagnosed for liver cancer had been treated as infected fallopian tube. Thank God I never stopped and thought it was my liver every time I felt the pain. I never did associate the pin with the death I was waiting for either. Life went as normal as we could pretend.

We rented a house for a few months in central Auckland. My genius husband had already engaged in purchasing land. Our home was built. On completion of our house I kept myself occupied by painting the whole interior myself. I took pleasure in the art of painting though that was my first. I could breathe easier not worrying about landlord finding out about me. The kids had settled in their new school.

Few months after my brush with hospital, I was pregnant; at least the test was positive. A second test at the elite women's hospital was also positive. "Do only bad sense of humor follow me?" I had silently questioned. I could not bear any more terminations and decided I would rather be sterilized. I instructed my doctor, and he instructed the surgeon at the women's hospital on my behalf. This is the only decision I had personally made regarding my body so far.

In the next follow-up visit, my GP informed me of the termination result. "The Women's National Hospital's report suggested that there was no sign of a fetus," he told me. I thought to myself, "What made me think I was pregnant? I did not have sex with my husband for a very long time." I left the doctor's surgery and headed back to the university where I had a psychology class.

My GP's clinic was a few minutes from the university. While driving, a wishful thought emerged. I had convinced myself that one day people who live with the virus will be able to have babies. I had appointed myself to be one of those, something I had not shared with my husband. I had felt that I owed my husband for those children I could not protect for him. One more child will give him peace of mind. Now I don't even have the organs; I got lost in the thought. "It's done, it's too late," I screamed loud as I drove inattentively down Symonds Street. A huge lump chocked my throat, tears running down my cheeks, and snot flowing into my mouth. "What have I done?" I screamed, crying very loudly. I suddenly reduced the volume when I noticed an old man in the next car watching me.

Pity that I had convinced myself that one day during my life, people like me will be able to have children I had thought to be be around and younger enough when drugs are available. Feeling sorry for myself was not going to help me that's when my mother's words of wisdom came to mind. You can never unscrumble scrumbled eggs, "Too late for that now," I thought. Go home and make sure the two you have are protected. For a very long time I grieved for those children I was never going to have.

One weekend we took a walk in Symonds Street when we spotted a shop called DaDa Africa Boutique specialized in African artifacts. Inside, I met Sharleen and Seidu. I had no idea meeting this couple on this day was going to open a whole new world. I was taken by Sharleen and her husband's genuine happy attitude. Intrigued by the hair style my daughter wore, she asked me if I could do that for a living. "There is a market for such styles but no one is offering such services," she disclosed. If I should consider this opportunity, I was to call her as she was going to help me start up. I called Sharleen within days. We had spoken over the phone a couple of times, and her excitement and energy had rubbed on me.

Within weeks I was finding it hard to cope with school work. Sharleen had made it her business to attract customers. I had started at two nights a week, then three, increasing to weekends. It was almost the end of my first university year, and business was looking good. One day Sharleen called me with news of a local and Australian magazine journalist wanting to interview me. Apparently, Sharleen had been noticed by everyone due to the new corn rowed hair style I had done for her. "It's the women's magazine," she had told me. I had no idea about why she was so excited. I just agreed to be interviewed. A week later, Sharlene showed me the magazine that had us in it and on the cover. "You have no idea how many people are calling to make appointments with Sophie's Choice," she explained.

Sophie's Choice was now my name. The magazine journalist had asked me of my name. I had said, "Sophie." She went on to add "s' choice" to the her article. I liked the sweetness sounds of it when I had register my bussiness Sophie'Choice was already a house hold.

Those times people did not acknowledge people who considered anything black culture as fashion. In my business that is what I was offering. I had opened a hair braiding studio that was attracting the young and the old. We turned any hair into sophisticated dreads. We weaved in colored extensions or a blend of several colors, and created sexy wearable night or day hairstyles. I was pleased to see my clients revolve from the young and old, rich and famous, the poor and the not-so poor. I had encountered parents, educators, caregivers, and employers who perceived that braids, hair extensions, and dreadlocks were for black people, and if not black then for poor or for those from somewhat dysfunctional families. That was understandable. This was new and foreign, and just like most things, people soon forgot and hoped that was going to pass over. I got to work with thousands of interesting people. I was very proud of what I had achieved. A lot of Kiwi kids were ready for a change in the fashion direction. I saw this as that. They would have done it twenty years prior to my services if someone had offered. With all that success, nothing was going to get me out of the dark world I was living in.

My work was one of my hiding places. I worked six days and the other one or two days in a month was to do whatever the kids wanted. I did live a normal life. That's the life everyone l presumed was leading. Everything I was doing were the duties I would have to do, dying or not. But, oh no, I still had to walk on a very fine line by pretending to be like everyone else. The everyday step that other people were taking for granted was a reminder of how different I was from everyone else.

While this was taking place in my life, Auckland city appeared to have been abducted overnight. The culture of the true-blue Kiwis was being invaded, and those who were accustomed to their way of living began to mumble, but it was too late. The young and those who gave change a chance were flourishing. I could not spiritually flourish as I was busy listening to what would be next. I listened to what would come and affect my hidden jungle.

New Zealand's story of the century was a story of a man called Peter Mwai. Driving home one evening I was listening to the radio news when the radio announcer said, "A man called Peter Mwai has been deliberately giving AIDS to women. If convicted he could face up to life in prison." I drove as fast as I could so I could catch the six o'clock national news. Sure enough I was not hallucinating. This story was on every news channel. Half an hour into the news, my knees were shaking. It felt like an earthquake was going to strike just my house. I could hear the skies rumbling with thunder, the daylight disappearing, and the scariest creatures coming to get my family.

Since the time I had been diagnosed with the disease, AIDS was not being spoken of. I was the first one as far as my brain was programmed. When the subject of AIDS was being broadcasted, it was always with the view that only black people and gay men contracted it. Unfortunately, this guy's story confirmed the theory that was being created behind this deadly disease.

His crime probably went into New Zealand's history as the most publicized criminal story. It did dominate headlines of every newspaper and magazine alike, posters in every street of every city in the country, and it also made world news. The country anticipated the consequences of this news with great interest. Comment from self-made doctors were flying all over. Some comments were definitely designed to frighten the sh—out of the human race. Most significantly fear was being induced, causing prejudice. For those who feed on prejudice and propaganda were using this as an excuse. I thought, "How dare you come here and mess up my life?" Yes, my life. I was very angry with Peter. I had thought I was the first and only one with the virus. I had been thinking that was the reason the government had kept me a secret. "Now that there is another African, does that mean the lid on what happened to me was to be lifted?" This thought alone hounded me. I became aware of all the things that were possible and how those things would affect my family in every way. "If I had ended up in Mwai's shoes, would my family's photos end up stuck on city buildings?" It was a thought I did not want to analyze.

For the New Zealand politicians to ensure that their people were safe, Peter was treated worse than war criminals who had killed entire populations. What was happening to Peter was a constant reminder of what was going to happen to me. Regardless of what we had done, we had one thing in common—we were both black and the pioneers of this disease in that country. As I watched the media painting a picture of this guy, I could not help thinking of what Peter was going through, and what I will be facing one day.

In my madness of describing the situation, analyzing how I was feeling, and attempting to diagnose my own symptoms, I came across this word, "paranoia." Paranoia is a disease in people like schizophrenics. I could swear I was never paranoid before this. I had never experienced this kind of feeling. Everything that I am was being perceived as contagious. I was experiencing a nasty feeling that was being easily triggered by a word, a look, even a thought. I was paranoid the minute I was next to someone who was either not one of my children or my doctor. Anyone else and I had to analyze what they might be thinking or would know before they even got closer. I had stopped being affectionate with anyone, including my children; nobody told me how contagious I was. As for my husband that was the end of our loving gestures.

Auckland had not turned to be a heaven for me, hell more like it. Now that people were talking about the virus, especially if you were black, I had known the meaning of paranoia when I looked up the symptoms but had no idea how to deal with the new added stress. Many times I had watched news in the company of other people regarding the virus. The news would state some new medical findings: "The University of Medicines in America has discovered a new drug for HIV sufferers. It won't be on the market for some time. Further tests are being conducted." It seemed as if I was the only person in the room who was listening to this. Sometimes I had remained on this subject well after the news, fantasizing about this miracle drug becoming available while I was still alive. Those who had been around had clearly by pass this it sometimes comment had been made such as, aren't you luck you are here. "Would you accept me if you knew who I am? I had thought silently. I came to realize that trying to be part of this society was just bribing my way into acceptance. With that, I dropped one by one of so-called friends and acquaintance. I did not want to have to cover up the paranoia which was getting worse the minute I opened my eyes."

I had no friends, but locking myself up was no option. "Go out, Sophie, and stop feeling sorry for yourself!" I told myself. I knew going out for a woman or man with rotten blood was illegal, but I did anyway only to learn some lessons. I had gone for a drink especially after work, always by myself. Every time I had gone for a drink, Mr. Good-looking-Smart-Intelligent had spotted me over the counter; comes and say, "What is a good-looking woman like you doing alone?" I knew he liked me, but there was something he wanted to say first, I had been in this situation before. Black people and gay men had been perceived as the cause of this deadly disease. I had the guts to even be seen in public while the Mwai story was a hit, not sure what I was thinking.

"Where are you from? How long have you been here?" As I gave this gentleman some answers I would think, "Here we go again, another ignorance of influence pick up line," then the conversation would continue, "You must be lucky to be here. There is a lot of AIDS over in Africa." On top of my lungs I wanted to ask, "Isn't it time you ask your government if there is AIDS here?" There! My night was spoiled. How can I be your friend when you have made your point already? I had gone home where my husband awaited me. I looked at my husband and felt sorry for him. I felt I had brought shame to our family. I was the wrong woman, now a woman that was carrying a killer disease. I was no longer feeling love for anyone, him or my kids. I felt isolated of which I began to believe I was an alien. Above all, life had been so cruel that nothing good came my way.

I walked out of my marriage. I don't know why or where I was going. I just wanted to be alone. For the first time, I felt stripped off everything I had left to live for. "What about my husband who was always proud of me? I am his best friend," I had thought to myself. I had to go, as I could no longer look at my husband and the kid's faces pretending we were family. In the narrow path of darkness I slipped into the world of silence, the world I was not prepared to live in. At this stage, I think I had lost strength, but something, someone else took over my body ready to carry on living.

I had been single for a while; even that was my secret. It had taken me few years to accept that singlehood was not a sign of failure but circumstances. At the beginning I would go for a drink after work always alone. I quickly noticed that single women who were on the move were not size eighteen. Soon after I lost all that weight I had put on from eating the good old Kiwi food. I became very extreme in my appearances. Bright, baggy shirts, jeans with cowboy shoes, and bright colored full double breasted suits borrowed from the UB40 vocal leaders' dressing style that I had envied. Those were the days girls drank B52s and tequilas while gorgeous men flaunted their sex cologne bodies. Unlike all other women of that time I was not an ordinary peacock. I had an X factor. I was a black girl in a white world and learning fast.

Being an outsider I became an expert at observing everything, from fashion trends to politics. I got the feeling that Auckland as a city was just getting sweeter and everyone wanted to party. Confident as I had become in my new skin, I surely leant a lot about city life and that was going to take a different turn—a turn which I took blindfolded.

The time I became a single mum, it was pretty much the beginning of the slow changing Auckland culture. With the immigration policy changing, I saw a few Africans, Middle-Eastern people, and Asians, including Indians, popping up mainly in the city. Most of the singles from the minority group did hang out in the night spots because that was the only way they could socialize. All this had created a new scene and exciting experience for many. I was very much part of the people who made the city attractive, fun, and dangerous. I had noticed that I stood out when strangers approached me with acknowledgments. I did stand out everywhere I went; that was not fun as it was an unwanted feature on my part. I must have developed some Whoopi Goldberg look-alikeness. Most times I had been referred to as Whoopi.

The fever of the city was about to present a twist in which I was not aware of. I had not thought anyone in this world would fancy me. One Friday night I met a man who was playing doctor on one of New Zealand television soap operas. I had been drinking at a bar across TV One studios in Victoria Street. I had hung out at this place with a friend named Angela. Angela had introduced me to most cool hangouts. It did not take long before I was streetwise. I had known how to get to these places alone after a while. I had the charm that went with the looks. When I had gone out of my bedroom, the first thing was to put on my mask, a mask made out of smile. I had presented myself with the same pose as normal people, and everyone seemed to be taken by that. I had come to understand that the mask was very much a portrait of the person inside, only if that person was not contagious.

The man was drop-dead gorgeous—tall, dark, and handsome. He used to drop me home after drinking with him all night. In the early hours of the morning, I found myself in Kohimarama, one of the well-groomed neighborhoods in Auckland city. Soon after we arrived at his flashy apartment, I found myself struggling to break the news as he began to undo my buttons. I could only say, "Please don't." His masculine voice asked, "Why not?"

And I struggled to spit the words out. The man forced himself lightly on me. After he had finished and poured me a glass of wine I found myself thinking, "Is that normal? What if it's not? Who would believe me?" I had not been raped, I knew that. I had let him kiss me and flirted with him all night. I had enjoyed, for ones I had enjoyed being desired by someone. I watched normal women looking at me with envy. What I had forgotten was I was not supposed to be around normal people, so I prayed for him.

As time went by, I figured out that this world was very complicated, more complicated than I had thought. Being black and alone, I could say I had my share of sexual consented abuse. It had been a while since I had listened to my womanhood sexually. When I had come to Auckland, I was a very different person. Few years later, I walked and talked like an Aucklander only felt like a criminal.

I was drinking more and more and hang out in night spots where no one would care. One day I had been out with a friend a few streets away from my shop. I noticed something that gives money and also sing. Upon asking my friend what that was, he told me it was a poker machine. He offered me a card loaded with money and showed me how to use it. I had never heard of a gambling machine. Most places I had been hanging out were situated at the Viaduct and city central. By the end of the evening, I had collected more than eight hundred dollars. It did not take long before I chose this place as a perfect place for me to relax after work. After a while, I was enjoying this so much that it became the only place I could find peace.

I had no sense of belonging. I had started losing what it was that made me Sophie. I was no longer enjoying my work just worked for the cash I need to put in the porker machine. At the beggining I had just spend ten dollars after work go home get ready and hit the city. I had no idea how I has stopped outing and just sit in front of the mechine all night. By this time I was spending upto five hundred every night.

Something rang a bell. I felt lost within, and the feeling of fear began to cloud over my head like a gathering storm. "What is going on?" I wondered, but it was too late—I had caught another strange disease. The jungle I had created in the big smoke was about to burn, and I could feel it closing in. With my new entertainment, I could see the changes in my behavior to that of someone else. The distraction that was now caused by gambling was starting to surface.

It was end of January 1997, Auckland anniversary day, when the winds of change showed up. I had known a girl called Jacqueline who originally came from Hawkes Bay. Usually we had catch up herd for a drink and dancing down town Auckland. While in the middle of dancing Jackie said "I am leaving for Hawkes Bay at 4:00 o'clock Sophie, you can come with me if you like. We will be back on Monday." As this was Auckland anivesary weekend, I took the opportunity to go somewhere new as I had not left Auckland since I had moved here. Even better, the kids were with their father as they aways has during school holidays.

At 4:00 a.m. we passed through my place, picked up a few things, and off we went to Hawkes Bay. Jack drove for the six-hour-trip while I slept off the alcohol. Jacqueline's parents lived in Hastings, a small place compared to Auckland. This was on a friday, the next two days, she took me for a drive, showing me the surrounding places. I suddenly said, "I like it here, Jackie. I will go home and bring back my kids as it was the beginning of school year." Jackie was surprised like everyone else she had no idea who the person she had come to love and respect was. I made sure I had visited the best school her mum had recommended. I visited the school and secured seats for my children. This was on a Monday, the last day of our long weekend.

Back in Auckland, I told the kids my new adventure. "We are moving to Hawkes Bay. It's a nice place, and I have found a good school. We will be staying at Jackie's parents' place till we found our own place," I told them. We packed essential things that could fit in the sports car and stored the rest of the household. We were off to our new destination within twenty-four hours. I had been always a good driver, and we all enjoyed the trip stopping every now and then for break. For a moment, it felt like I had escaped from the demons.

Mum as usual makes it look so easy because they will have a roof over their heads and a guard that looks after them. We enjoyed the hospitality of Jackie's family and soon we found our own place. I managed to start my business over again and settled the kids in school. I had left Auckland at the drop of a pin and did not prepare on how I was going to start again. I did not remind myself of the reasons I could not live in Edgecumbe and why Auckland was the best place for me.

With the changes in my world, so also my behavior, I soon began to recognize behavior that I was never accustomed to. I was lucky I had been very well the last few years I had been in Auckland. It took me by surprise when one day I fell ill. As I needed a doctor, I chose to visit one at a nearby town of Napier, which was a ten-minute drive. On my way a friendly reminder from a mystery voice said, "Do you understand no one would understand your secret?" I gave it a thought and missed Auckland for a moment, then made a decision. I was not going to use my real name,

I had decided. On treatment I was asked for a blood test, but I never went back again. I came up with a new idea when I could not shake whatever was eating me. This time I managed to get antibiotics without too many investigations at a different clinic. I am in a different town, but I am still a criminal, I had thought sadly.

Soon I was to learn to live with pain. Simple tasks like a headache, It was a task that I had to consider if worth humiliation. The pain would have to last for weeks, dreading the trip to visit the doctor. There were situations where I had to go to the doctors if I wanted to work the next day. When I had arrived at the doctor's clinic, I became somewhat of an overstayer; that's how I felt. Nervous as a rate, felt like a thief, wondering if anyone has recognized me or are they my neighbor, if the patient sitting next to me is my children's teacher or friends' parent. When its time to declare my details, I had to lie on one question. "Do you have illness related to HIV?" I stared at it for a minute, then skipped; my heart was used to do the skipping the minute I heard the word AIDS or seeing it. I knew if I wanted to be treated well, I had to say no.

On one occasion I had wanted to have just one doctor who would know my secret, so I could get appropriate treatment. On this occassion I waited till I was inside his office, I said, "Doctor, there is something I did not declare. I am HIV positive." Confidently, he picked up his pen to write something on my file. He then walked toward a cabinet, pulled a pair of gloves, put them on, and started to examine. His body language seemed to say, "Please do not sneeze." "I have to do some tests," the doctor explained. I began to miss Auckland; at least I had a doctor there. I had gone home and not bothered to get the tests done.

The reason was I knew I had an infection that needed be treated. How was this possible? With desperation, I had gone to a different doctor and not declared my existing condition. The doctor felt no need of gloves and treated me for what I said hurt. I would get a prescription of antibiotics. I had always informed my dentist of my condition because there was a lot of blood in their work. I had lived with a very painful tooth as a result of this. While waiting for my turn, I could see the dentist's assistant discussing my declaration form. A patient behind me got called first, then another. "Hey, my appointment was forty-five minutes ago?" I had asked politely.

"I am sorry. The dentist is very busy. He cannot do it today, but there is another place you can try."

I knew I was not a stupid. I just had to live with an unacceptable disease that terrified people, even those that chose to save lives. No one had stopped and thought how miserable my day was going to be. They had assumed that their tactics of refusing me treatment had worked. I remember a friend saying, "They can't do that. You have to write a letter and complain." "Where do I start complaining?" I had thought to myself. This is a system that is designed to embrace the desirables and to ignore the unfortunate. Meanwhile, the only people who knew the secret I carried seemed to have forgotten to warn me of what was to come if I was not to die. For some reason, I created a home remedy called "a bit of Dettol in a glass of water will help kill the stomach bug." If a pain can give way because of Panadol, why worry? I don't need a doctor for that.

I had turned to marijuana as a tranquillizer pill. I could not believe how my life had changed from living on the side of the desired citizens to I charming up to those I had perceived as the undesirable citizens. It wasn't the small and sunny town that was different I had changed, I was very different from who I was. I had met a lady through my work and became friends. Most afternoons when the kids had gone to school, she would come and pick me up, and together we would visit her friends. In a large garage, we had gathered around a large table. Cups of coffee were emptied and the old herb readily rolled would be brought out from handbags and bras. This was a place and time for women only. It was great to be part of those moments and I envied these women so much. If only they could see what was really sitting in front of them. During this time I slowly learned to smoke as my friend had suggested, "If you are finding sleeping hard, you might need a little smoke after work." Slowly, I learned to smoke. I was paranoid for the first couple of months. I was thinking if I got caught smoking, all my secrets would come out. As time went by, the benefits were greater, and the paranoia disappeared; Also some of the prejudice I had lived with diminished, What my friend did not know was I had lost half of my family and never been allowed to repeat the words. I had thought so much of my babies, and they started visiting me in my dreams, mostly around the month of May, when I would think how old they could have turned. "Thank God there are illegal drugs that actually make people like me laugh and have a good night's sleep, I had appreciated".

One evening as I drove my car out from the parking at a local pub, I was stopped by the police. It was the first time that I got into trouble with the law. I had had too much to drink and failed the test. The cops took me to the station and took my photo and told me to attend the court the following week. I had never gone out of my way to get into trouble. I always had a sense of duty. On my court day, I went to the courthouse nicely dressed. I was trying to separate me from those I had perceived as criminals. Besides, I was the only black person in the area, how I was being ashamed. After I had been given community service of sixty hours, I went home.

The following week I began to serve my time. I had to clean a tennis club restaurant and the tennis court areas. I did not know I could not handle some of the work the manager was making me do. With that I called a lawyer so I could change community work for fines. Another court date was set up. On the day, the Judge called my name and my lawyer was to speak on behalf of me.

All I could hear was "We can't charge her if her name is not in the system." My lawyer told me I was dismissed because the police did not have my records. "Someone is looking after me," I said. "Did someone recognize my name and got me out of the situation before people find out whom I am? Is it possible that the people that had the opportunity to practice their evil powers on my family were watching me?" I was only walking back in time, only this time consciously, and one by one the past events began to surface. "Do things like this happen to me only, or does this happen to everyone? How is it that my name got lost? Am I in the system? If so what is my status to date with the law?" Obviously, I was talking to myself. "You can't ask those questions, Sophie. Just pray someone is looking after you. You are not in a position to complain. Are you willing to risk the few years you have left for your children to reach adulthood?" It's that voice again talking to me. Every day was another day for me. A beer and a game of pool with the boys suited me just fine. Strange enough that is. Most people who got to know me envied me while some thought I was lucky, when they came to know that I got off my charge because my file had got lost.

I had adjusted the big city behavior I had acquired to suit this small community. What could have been hard about dressing a little down, putting on less make up, and carrying a happy face with no traces of pain. Gradually, I discovered that each place had its own type of rock and roll. That required an expert to fit in, especially when you are the only black face. I had come here to rest and to reevaluate my life unconsciously. Consciously I was only thinking about staying anonymous, not mysterious. My business had improved enough to support my habit that was still lingering.

As a person who had other hidden talents, I could also play pool. At night, the locals came to play pool at the pub after work. I became part of the club and enjoyed meeting new friends. One night, a man that had been watching me play pool all night challenged me. I was happy to contest my position and his bet was to win me. I lost the game and he won. He won me for the night but that turned out to be the beginning of a relationship. I could not get rid of him as he was from out of town. It did not take long before the relation turned abusive.

A month or two had gone by, and he wanted more than a condom between us. As the drama I had always dreaded began to unfold, the name calling turned into physical. I did not feel him and was the opposite of a man I could chose if I had a choice. I had thought it was OK to save the bet but could not disclose my illness. He went too far, and I had no one to tell. Something had clicked in his mind why our sex life was unsatisfactory. When I had thrown him out of my place, he had been gone for two weeks but was still calling me. I had thought he got the massage, so he won't abuse me if I took him back. A big mistake. I had not learned the rule that "an abuser is always an abuser." When I had to collect his dirty washing, I checked one of his pants he had been wearing the day he came back. In it I found a clinic blood result. I was shocked to know he had gone as far as checking himself to know if he had caught AIDS from me. I stole the result and kept it. The many times he had forced himself on me he should surely have gotten the disease. Thank God he was negative. The abuse resumed after a few days of coming back. I knew I had no rights. I could not tell the police. At the end he left me with untreated concussion. One evening when he had drunk so much he head butted me. I did not see a doctor till I could not stand the dizziness I was having. My brain would swell and the bed felt as if it was spinning ten times the speed of a car. I had to see someone. I lied to the doctor why I was so. Thankfully my friend Pamela came and rescued me from this man. I had never been rescued from a relationship or been on the receiving end of an insult every weekend.

I moved to Napier. Napier was a small city but elegant. It is known for its art decor and wine industry. I had reestablished my business, and Karl Baker was a thing of the past. I had not learned much even with the experience I had had with Karl that had demaged my head. Later I met a person I thought was the love of my life. He was nice, loving, and everything a woman needs. For the first time I felt I had someone. During this time, I was struggling with gambling. Although Timothy, the new boyfriend, was a nice guy, he could not help me with my problems. We both liked luxurious lifestyle, while we both had no skills to balance the two. We built our relationship based on that and were very happy; at least he was.

I had felt for a while what life should feel like. Somehow there was the other mind that reminded me of who I was. Nevertheless, I did not know what to do with the secret. I was not about to change that, so I took a gamble. We got engaged after a year, and he was happy and I was happy.

One time I experienced something that reminded me of my past dreams, something I had not wanted to think about in years. We had visited a friend of ours. She lived in the countryside on the old highway from Napier to Wellington. She had wanted to take us sightseeing not far from where her rural house was. After she had been driving for a little while, she stopped to show us an old church that stood alone. There was nothing much around it except a view of small hills and a gorge below.

Here I was confronted by a familiar view. As she was telling me the history of the first settlers that built the little old church that stood by itself in the middle of nowhere. I could hear partially what my host was saying. I had been consumed by memories of my previous journey to this place. "I have been here" was the feeling that filled me. I was trying to remember why I had flown over this place in my dream. What is it that I was supposed to see? "Chased by horrible things in all my dreams, I had always been able to escape by flying away, and one of those places was real," I thought sadly. I did not know if my friend noticed. Immediately, the fear of remembering my dreams struck and I quickly returned my focus to my friend's kindly guided tour. Every time I had thought of this visit, I had gotten a funny feeling, an almost scared feeling. As I was good at not letting myself being caught up self-pitying, I carried on with the relation I was in and with my work.

Few years down the road, my problem to gambling just got worse, and my partner felt he was going down with me. No matter what I tried, I ended up there so blinded with my other problems. I became a loser. One thing I was not expecting was stress. It was agonizing, yet I couldn't get out. Devastated by all this, I lost my self-esteem and felt ashamed and wished the world should crash down on me at once. It was painful. It felt like a slow death, slow death on top of another slow death. I was so tired. "I am supposed to be a strong and intelligent person. How could I be so stupid?" I would curse myself. Normally those words would only surface when I could not find a tear drop. The dysfunctions were becoming obvious.

I began to feel like a skeleton that was fighting to keep its bones. My jungle was starting to show some gaps. This time it was not so much of the jungle, I was worried about. It was becoming apparent that I was running away from something. The relation with Tim had turned into disaster, the disaster I had also predicted. I was feeling powerless and idealess at the same time. I was worried about my children finding out about what was really happening. What about the man I was with that I loved with all my heart. In that heat my partner felt the ugly side of my life; somehow I pushed him away. He was giving so much love not just to me, but to my kids as well. I knew what I had to do to make things better for our loving relation; even that was too much to sacrifice. There was nothing in any part of my body that daydreamed about coming out of the closet. If I had known that loving was not so simple, I would never have put me in that position. The very same year my children left home, my youngest now seventeen, to live with their father in Auckland. It did not take long for the man I had been engaged to to move out. By now the feeling of something big was going to happen hounded me. I just didn't know what that was.

Alone and scared, the drinking and the gambling kept me company. One day I met a man that I had never thought I will meet. As it turned out I did. In this town I had heard of a person I called "interesting" way before I moved here.

One morning while living in Auckland, I was listening to the radio news as I drove to work. My favorite subject popped up: "A man in Hawkes Bay has been giving women the AIDS virus that he contracted while on holiday," the radio said. As usual I took interest to find out what happened to him; instead, nothing more was ever said again. A few days later, I assumed that the media had thought if this story went too far it would overshadow the story of a black man called Peter Mwai that was making big headings then.

Somehow, for years, I remembered the story not thinking I would ever be in the same town where the story took place. One day when I had finished with my ex-fiance I met the man that I was never to forget. The guy was a mirror image of me—likable, sexy, calm, and definitely had the X factor when it came to women. I had met him a couple of times at the pub where he was working. We had instantly liked each other. On the first date we had a few drinks and then headed to his place. I was never a person to go to someone's house the first night, but he had insisted while passing my house that was a few meters from the pub. Nothing was fishy. As far as I was concerned, I liked him.

The only thing I remembered the next morning was him offering me a beer before going to bed, and it was almost untouched on the bedside table when I woke up. I woke up knowing that I had participated in sexual activities that I would normally think twice about. Whatever had caused that, I somehow enjoyed the evening with him. When warmed up to each other, I asked for protection, weird that I already knew we did not use them the previous hours. "Whatever you have I have got it by now," he replied as if it was OK with him. Even so I felt I had nothing to lose after taking a liking to his charm with that attitude. That morning something about his health rang a bell. He had a nasty cough that sounded like TB or something quiet bad. It is then I remembered the story on the radio I had heard years earlier and thought he could be the man I heard on the radio years back

This was just a weeks before Christmas. My son and his girfriend had come to spend christmas with me. On Christmas day, I invited him to my house for Christmas lunch. I had been to his house before Christmas day to a party and had lots of fun. I never saw him again until two weeks after New Year. He looked battered, and this confirmed what I had suspected the first morning I stayed at his place. He told me he had been in hospital and been diagnosed with hepatitis. The radio story I had heard years ago flashed back. I knew where he was with the virus, especially with the lifestyle he was leading. I was yet to learn about another person's struggle. "How bizarre!" I had thought.

A few days later, a middle-aged woman walked into my shop while I was dreading a young man's hair. She asked if I was Sophie. When I had confirmed, she said, "I am coming from Dr. X's clinic. A man has . . ."—before she finished that sentence my worse fear reloaded—"told the doctor you gave him the AIDS." I asked her to come outside with me and later visited that doctor. I found out that that man had been in hospital with full-blown AIDS, as they used to describe the last days of an HIV-virus patient. I askedd the doctor how possible is that he is dying after one night and a week later. After the doctor had send me for blood test my result came back, Its then I felt relieved when he had told me that this guy had the virus way before I met him. Although relieved, my worst fears had just been confirmed. I had lied to the doctor when he asked me of having any knowledge that I was positive. How lucky could this guy be? This guy has lived in this area for a long time, has been a DJ, rave organizer, has worked in a record shop, and as a bartender he is well known. He did not wait for my results. He just went and told the whole town why he was dying.

If shame could kill, I could have then, but I had no choice but to carry on living. That was wishful thinking. With people whispering and some openly asking questions, I knew I was not going to survive this one, but I was not going to run. Even if I wanted to run, I could not have been able to. I was that tired. Suddenly, I was getting visits from women I had never heard of, some of them from as far as the capital city. It was comforting but also too late. They were to see for themselves the person that had caused all their pain. I will never know what he really said to them; at least they also had some closure, I had thought. Sad, after thirteen years, I was still convinced that I was the only one in this town if it was not for this guy. I am not sure if he is the man I heard on the radio; he surely had the resemblance of him. I was lucky enough to be his victim in order for him to come out of his closet. I was not angry but happy that I was part of his way to exile. While trying to comfort myself with that idea, I could not believe he had called three women who were affected to give them closure of how that came by.

I had long come across the thought of people living in closet before I met this guy. One evening I had gotten a call from a best friend; she was frantic. She had pleaded I go to her house; she had something to tell me. It was no use asking her to tell me over the phone. I said, "Look, I can't get there as I had a few drinks." Not sure what she was going to tell me, I remained worried just from what I sensed from her voice. We met at lunchtime at my shop the next day and quickly closed the doors. She looked washed and clearly didn't know what to say, and her tears poured uncontrollably. She finally had the strength to tell me what the doctor had said about her results. We hugged tightly, and I told her everything was going to be all right. "What am I going to do, Sissy?" she said as she sobbed. "I wish I knew" was my secret reply. Instead I promised to be there for her as I understood what she was going through. I could not tell her who I was, so my promise to her felt short of a deceit.

Only shadows do survive to see the light, the story of my life. People had said to me, "You have lived quite an interesting life. You should write a book." I am a person you could find in any place and will find a story to talk about. I had a beer in a British pub and talked about being half British. Just to find myself entertaining strangers as I let them know I inherited that through my education system. I had jocked about being Irish because I could drink a pint of Guinness in no time. I can eat black pudding and I enjoy St Patrick's Day. I have hobbies and interests that aren't lady like but a lady in always. I had always been a person who could tell half my life story in twenty minutes. Sometimes people had asked, "How old are you?" Obviously I might have said a lot. Occasions like these had always reminded me of the other half of my life that I never shared.

The story they were referring to would have featured only the good parts I wanted them to know about me, not what was beneath. However, it seemed to have been a good idea; I had wanted to express my feelings one way or another. As for writing a book, I could not see the purpose in it if no one was going to read it. Even though I had considered writing as a cry for help, I feared that language was going to be a problem, because my childhood did not allow me to study long enough to reach a higher level. I had dismissed these comments as just pub talks. From just that thought I knew I would never write a story, any story. Besides, those people who made comments like these barely knew the real me. I wondered had I told them the other half of my life, what they would have said. Would they have encouraged me to write?

It is thanks to these people who could see a story in me that I mustered the courage to write. One of them was a guy called Tim, "Tim the Irishman," as I called him. I met Tim in an Irish bar while living in Napier. I had been living there for nearly four years, regularly hanging out at the Irish pub most weekends. I had not met anyone foreign or thou many Foreigners visited Napier for its famous Art Décor, Food and Wine festivals. As it turned out he was one visitor to Napier that was meant to be my mentor for life.

Somehow I had always been attracted to people like me who had a story to tell. As it happened, Tim was not one of them. He was one of the good strangers I did meet. Tim the Irishman seemed to have been searching for something from the stories he had told me. He was a storyteller and probably a mind reader. I had wondered after, spending the afternoon With Tim at my little flat I lived just a minute from the old Napier hospital. I had revised what he had said to me over and over again. He had touched on certain things that no one had ever dared say to me. He had made me shiver with fear; how much does he know? Also a strange but scary question, "How much of my skeletons are starting to show?" Oh! He had already asked me what I was running away from. How I can forget that?

The day before he left for Ireland, Tim came back to my place and gave me a bookshop receipt. He had taken time to go search for the book that he had recommended called *Bird by Bird*. When finding that the shop did not have it in stock, he ordered the book and paid for it. It was very nice to have met Tim, but was he just a foreigner I met at a pub or a messenger? I had not thought about that yet except that every time I read my diary entry that I had written the day he visited my place. It reads: Tim said, "Look in the mirror. You will find all you are looking for. If you don't see anything, keep looking." Even just an entry in my diary would cause a chill that ran through my spine. The chill would cause a panic, followed by me looking around to see if someone was watching me. How had Tim noticed how scared I was? He had said, "I can see you are scared."

Having this entire incident happening one after another was taking a big chunk of me. Summer 2001 I closed my business and I solated myself even from the only thing that gave me freedom. Now unemployed for the first time in my life, I had only the gambling outlets entertaining my poor soul. The Greg saga had long gone to many forgetful minds. My struggle for air was increasing. No situation seemed to improve. I became very alonely, sad and scared. I could feel the nakedness of living without my shadow.

I got a phone call from a friend who lived in Auckland asking me to visit her and have a break. I had shared the grief of being lonely to her, mostly about the breaking up with Tim. Somehow I knew something was wrong. At this stage I knew something very wrong was about to happen. I was not well. It was end of October 2001, just after I had met Tim the Irishman. I was not only tired, I had had the heaviest period ever. I had clearly grown leaner, and my skin shade had darkened quiet significantly. I took the opportunity to go visit my GP. At the same time, I was in Auckland. As I was busy helping my friend, I went to see my GP the last week of my stay. I had been in Auckland for four weeks not feeling well.

The last time I had visited him was roughly nine years prior to this day. He said, "You are looking very well." And I said, "Did you think I was dead, Doctor?"

He gave me a wonderful grin acknowledging what I had meant. I described how I was feeling in reply to him inquiring about my health. He performed an intense examination as if he was compensating for those years he hadn't seen me. I don't blame him. The last time I had seen my GP, I was still Mrs. Someone. He hadn't known that my family had a breakup, for earlier in those years ago he had arranged a counselor to help save my marriage.

My GP could have guessed why I had come all the way back to see him in the state I was. I had just told him how things had been after the breakup. I had also indicated I had had no doctor during the period he hadn't seen me. As he prepared a blood test form, he insisted I had done it that very same day. I immediately remember the last time when he had sent me to Auckland Hospital straight from his clinic. I did not wait for the result; instead, I flew back to Napier.

TIME TO REFLECT AND A WINDOW TO EXILE

*E*verything I had done I had to plan normally in the shortest time, probably not found in the Book of Guinness. On this occasion, someone had decided what and where I was to be. Maybe I was too slow or I had run out of ideas, but to be honest, at this stage I had stopped feeling. I knew there was something coming that was more apprehensive than I could handle, and it felt like it was meant to be. I had not thought I would end up in hospital.

My GP called me with the results and urged me to fly back to Auckland Hospital if possible the very same day. His nurse's voice was filled with urgency, especially after I told her how sick I had become the last week. I flew into Auckland city straight to the hospital. Boy, was I sick. A swelling the size of a little tennis ball stored under my skin just below my left chin. My bed was ready in the ninth floor and my name tag on the door. Clearly, my GP had found something more serious than he said over the phone. "You had to go to the hospital. All the arrangements had been made. Go straight to ward nine." That echoed in my ears as I thought of how I was going to get there. I had been broke after for some time after I had blown all my savings to gambling. Rohan, my ex-husband, came to my rescue when I had asked if he could buy me a ticket to Auckland, pick me up, and drop me at the hospital. When Rohan had looked at me, I saw what he was thinking; he looked worried. Temperatures were running forty plus degrees. I had no appetite, felt weak, and sleepy.

After what seemed to be hours waiting in the long large corridors, a nurse who had asked me to sit on a sofa came back and showed me to my room.

I had been given a room with a view of the Auckland central city. The room was designed for one bed, a toilet, and a shower. There was a television on the wall, and below was a sofa and a trolley. A bedside lamp, two drawers on one side and on the other, emergency bell and machines fitted on walls. A long curtain hanged alongside my bed. At this point, the stigma of the disease I have had wake up, on its feet and now walking, thats the feeling I got. "No one in this hospital would like to be sharing a room with someone with my virus," I thought for a second. Honestly, I preferred it that way, so I dismissed the thought. The smell of this room was more of toilet cleaning chemicals that were diluted with medicines, and somehow, I could smell what I thought was a combination of diseases and death. I don't know how I reached this conclusion, but it wasn't pleasant. My comforting thought was that this was going to be my room till the doctors found out what was wrong with me.

Within a short time, blood tests were being conducted, nurses were preparing my hand for drips, and somehow I was there as an observer. This did not seem to be happening to me. Something in me seemed to have identified the situation and felt like it was long due. I just wanted to sleep, and for the nurses to stop taking temperature, blood pressure, and heart rate every half hour. After the doctors had written notes and retire for the day, my ordeal had just started.

It's the experience and the happenings that so much fascinated me as if I saw it in a movie. It is also a place in my life that I experienced the visibility of miracles. This was December 18, 2001, the end of the run, I had thought, when I was lying in Auckland Hospital. I have also named this period, "time to reflect and a window to exile."

I had very little blankets on my bed, that night I felt the west of high temperatures. I was so cold I never felt this cold even my winter days in Gisborne did not compare. "I am cold, nurse," I said with my teeth chattering. The nurse brought me painkillers to reduce temperature and remove some blankets off me. I thought that was strange. Couldn't she hear what I said. "I am cold," I said. "Just relax, you are only feeling cold.

It's the temperature, but you need less blankets," the nurse had replied. I could not understand the logic in that. So sick I would try to relax, as I allow my body to relax, I felt warm then warmer till all the sheets were wet from sweating. My brain was trying to analize if this is how people with AIDS face their final days.

I had always thought hospitals were spooky and scary, especially at night. I had never wanted to imagine myself in a spooky place. At the time I was lying in my bed, I did not think or get scared. I came to understand that the spooky part I had imagined every time visiting hospitals is what was to happen to me. This place was here for a reason. You either die or get well. If you die, this will became your last place to have lived. I did not know what was going to happen to me. Whatever the outcome, I wasn't afraid anymore. I came to understand one part of imagination. Imagination is not reality nor can it be compared with experiencing.

Too sick and too tired, I manage to sleep half the night with nurses coming in and out to check and offer painkiller if I needed any. It had been almost a week and a half since I had eaten well. I had been sick for a while before the day I was admitted. Nothing had changed this first morning. I was not hungry. Hospital food was designed to keep people going; it was not an appetizer. I tell you what: I open my breakfast that had been placed at my trolley. The tray had a big silver lid that was attractive. When I opened it, there was a piece of cold unbuttered toast, a little butter, jam, cooked porridge that looked cold, a little milk, and a sachet of sugar. I put the lid back and waited for the doctor to come; it was almost ten o'clock before a doctor came in.

The doctor that came in had a familiar face, I noticed, as he greeted me. "Hello, Sophie, how are you?" I greeted him back politely. "I am Doctor Pegler. It has been a long time since I saw you." I remembered him as the doctor that had looked after me the first time I was admitted in the early nineties. I felt a bit at ease to be attended by someone who knew who I was. After a physical examination, he left. When he returned, he told me

I was going to have blood transfusion. I must have been anemic for a long time, I had thought. "A biopsy specialist will come and see you tomorrow. The nurses will look after you," he added as his body gesture indicated his time with me was over. I looked at him and spoke with a soft voice. All I could say was "OK, OK" and "thank you." When he walked out, drew the curtains open, all I could do was cover my face with my palms. Hot tears poured, and I sobbed myself to sleep.

It was a very short sleep as the next thing I heard was "Are you awake, Miss?" And I had my first blood transfusion. I learnt my blood type, a positive side of being near death. I don't know anyone who has experienced as many blood tests in life as I did. The days that followed I had blood test every morning, sometimes twice when doctor had time to discuss other results. This felt like buckets and buckets of blood were being drained out of my veins. I could never wish to be treated by anyone other than the doctors from the infectious department in Ward 9. I looked awful. I probably hated this part more than the fact that I was an infected person with a deadly virus.

I had always strived to have the best acceptable appearance for more than one reason. Most important was to bribe acceptance. A team of doctors and staff were dedicated to see me through whatever I was facing. I could feel and see that with all my heart. I had never imagined being in this place, yet I was at peace with myself and accepting what was to come. I felt like I was home after being in a war zone for a very long time.

"Your situation is complicated." My hospital doctor and head of department had informed me one morning when I had suggested to him that I needed another blood transfusion. I had already had two transfusions by then and felt very little difference. The most buzzer thing about the blood thing, I physically felt thirsty for more blood when I suggested this to him.

I had a lump under my chin on the right side. No one knew what to do with it. This lump had formed a week before I was admitted and had grown to the size of a tennis ball overnight. The confusion among doctors was scary but managed to see the funny side of it. I had been in hospital for a week and half the doctor who was supposed to operate had not seen any results on what it was. Thank God he was late. On arrival he arranged for another X-ray. An hour later, a doctor on duty told me I was not to be operated on as the test had shown the lump was disintegrating on its own. In the past I had never consciously associated any symptoms as "going to be the cause of death." The minute I felt the lump and the time it took to develop, I did believe the lump on my neck was the one. When the results showed the state of the lump, I heaved a sigh of relief as I liked the results very much. I knew my body had responded to something, especially when my doctor had come in the next day praising the outcome. Two weeks on, the lump had gone and the skin on my neck was peeling off.

Normally I never was one to expect much when it came to luck. I had lived a fast life. This time I knew what positive meant. During the investigation my doctor had found a virus bacterium, and he was trying to find out if it was TB. Every method used to test tuberculosis was applied. For each method used was repeated two to three times. This was the only negative so far in my life. And as it was a concern he wanted to find what that bacterium was. Meanwhile, I was put on TB medication. Typical of my character, I took the medicines home and avoided taking them, a week later I ruturned them with a form that I had been givern to sign if I should not want to take them.

Meanwhile the smear test result from my GP was abnormal. Then a second test was conducted by the hospital was also abnormal. It was time for a specialized test from the women's hospital. It definitely confirmed I had cancer of the womb as far as I was told. While on trial treatment and test of other things that was going wrong, I was placed on an emergency waiting list for hysterectomy. Women's hospital was a good ten minutes away from the hospital, and I was going to be taken there by the hospital transport. I am only glad I was used to telling nurses I was HIV positive. In this place they were not used to this word (my guess). After the operation, I was glad I could walk again. I was so skinny by this time that I used to cry each time I caught the reflection of my skinny figure.

I went back to Auckland Hospital and was glad I was back where everyone knew my name. I had been in the hospital for nearly four months. One afternoon, I received a letter with the operation results. It stated no cancer cells but found granules. "It's just another mistake. You did not have cancer." I had re-enacted the message to myself silently. I had to confirm this with my junior doctor when he visited my room the next morning. I was in a very different mood that I wondered if he had noticed. Normally, I had always charmed up on him entering the room. He was the youngest doctor and very sexy. After he had examined my stitched tummy, I said, "Do these kind of things happen just to me? Does anybody understand how it feels to have all your inside taken out and then someone comes and say 'oops!'?" I stopped what ever I wanted to say next as I felt the lump of pain blocking my swallowing tubes.

"At least you don't have to worry about having that kind of cancer," he replied with his usual soft comforting voice. "It's not the point," I said angrily, turning my head the opposite direction. He wished me a good day and left. The familiar hot tears slowly ran down my cheeks. That's when it really hurt.

Let me describe one scenario that no one ever told me. I know people grieve when they lose their loved ones. I know people cry of pain when they have a caesarian birth but rejoice the outcome. What I did not know is when parts of us are removed, it is a personal funeral. I did not sleep for months. I cried as if I had lost someone to death. Losing my body parts and staying alive was worse than if I had just died.

There is nothing in my world called "you can never get used to pain." Believe me, you can if you don't kill yourself. Something will never stop hurting. For me it is the scars of pain that I would not like to disappear. It is part of me, and it should not be described as pain.

While in hospital, I was discovering myself. Only I did not know what to expect next. I had the opportunity to know people on a friendly basis. For the first time in many years, I felt the feeling of being myself. I felt like part of me, the dirty part that I was so ashamed of, no longer had a hold on me. I had had cleaning ladies come and talk to me. One older Maori nurse would come and visit me when she started her shift at eleven. She had spent more time than a nurse's visit for a checkup and medication. I had cherished her extra effort as she reminded me of my people when it came to caring for others.

I had made friends with other patients. Once I went for Sunday mass as one of the patients had suggested. I did not want to go but had to be polite. Visiting God's room to me seemed to be jumping the gun. I did not know what to say to him. One thing I knew was he was watching over me. As I entered the chapel, I felt a strange feeling. It was as though God had ignored me, telling me, "Don't bother coming in here. I am not ready for you yet." I did not know how I interpreted the feeling into those words in the shortest time I had sat in the chapel. At the end of the service, I was convinced that God had spoken to me, asking me to restore my faith. Anything that was positive at this time was better than me crying for the life I had not lived.

I was so tired that it was nice to have someone doing something for me for a change. I was watching my doctors trying to revive me back to life. While drifting away, I could still feel that someone had a hold on me, and I was not so alone. Many times I had put my five senses into helping the doctors see I was not about to give up. My doctor would jokingly say, "You are a difficult case," or "Well, stop playing doctor until you see me." At times, I was so full of life, but there was something missing the minute I felt better. I was more peaceful in the half-dead status I was in as I was in no-man's-land. Feeling better was as scary as dying, and leaving my family behind was the saddest of all.

The darkest time was when I was trying to prepare for the final exit consciously. The world looked like a perfect picture, yet my world was dark, lonely, and scary like a room with no windows. I was suffering from fear which had control over my life. I was scared of losing my family, and at the same time I had no world to share life with if God should have mercy on me. There is nothing as scary as death in life, probably scary when that's all you had to think about. In order to blend with the society, I laughed outside while crying inside.

I had a daydream where I had foreseen my kids and their father burying me at a cemetery, then walk away. I could feel the sadness in them all, and I would wonder "how on earth are they going to cope without me?" Now alone, buried, and realizing my body would decompose and the maggots will then take care of me, I had freaked out with fear. With that thought I had made a plan on what I had wanted to happen when I die. One important thing was my resting place. I wanted them to carry my ashes wherever they went until one of them died and then be buried together. Though still alive I could see that even in spirit I was going be a scared, lonely, and miserable soul. Who has been given a chance to face death and make choices, as scary as it is? I did at times and felt a whole lot better about the fact that the hospital had been a blessing in disguise.

I had accepted the hospital as my home; Christmas had come and gone, so had the New Year. Now in 2003, I am in and out the hospital mainly going home for a few days and back again sometimes as an emergency case. I had a permanent room where I was always sent to. There was no sign of me leaving this place. I had no time for sympathy or prejudice, nonsense that I had been previously occupied with. All I was asking for was respect if this was my last resting place. When this was happening, I was learning to accept a few more situations allowing me to focus on looking after me.

While being hounded by the prospect that there was no place for me outside the establishment that I was confined to, I had been able to wander around the hospital grounds. On a nice day I would grab a towel and lie down in the museum gardens that were situated by the hospital. Had anyone ever gone through grief and think, "how did all this start, what do I do, and why me, for that long and not getting anywhere? I could hardly see the ducklings floating happily in the nearby pond. I was busy staring at distant buildings, trying to analyze what my life was going to be the next day, and I would draw a total blank. When I tried to make sense with one thing the other did not correspond. I was back to square one. Slowly, I would walk back to my ward emotionless.

There was a big change in the way I was processing the information that occupied my mind. I had a voice that accompanied me and a lot of information to process. I would stand on my hospital window that looked over the city every day, hoping to see a different view. Instead my thought would revert inside my life. "What is that eating me? Who was I before all this? I had lost the person I was, and the person I was had to be brought back to life. That person had to come back to life." Those words would echo endlessly. "And how do I do that?" Many time I had thought about the "how" word. I would answer to this saying, "Just go to a psychiatric hospital, Sophie. That's where you belong." However, another voice would say, "But if you really think you are not crazy, how are you going to cope in such an environment?" It's that voice again having a conversation with me. I had conversation after conversation with myself, and most times that voice was appreciated when it butted in.

Months had gone by. I was feeling as though someone was looking after me. I had less stress, less worries, and life was easier as if there would be no hunger and the rain would never stop. I did not have to wake up every morning and say where to and who I was. For a change everything was being taken care of by someone else. Where should I be going to was now the creator's command.

I had been told that "you have to take the first step and admit that you are addicted." A gambling counselor had told me this when I had looked for help while living in Napier. That did not work. I had become one of those patients that were allowed to leave the hospital for walks or home on weekends if I needed a break from the hospital environment. During walks into town, I would gamble for an hour, then go back to the hospital. Somehow, this was the only entertainment I could have from my death bed. How sad, I had thought. Although I hadn't gambled for some time, I knew I was still an addict. Every day that passed I reminded myself that gambling was not the reason I lay half dead in hospital. Something must have shed a light for me to think this way.

Gambling is a disease inflicted by greedy people. Because when people forget to stop and think, they are really in trouble. I knew trouble is where I already was. I never stopped to think what all that was about. What I had recognized was stress caused by addiction was an addition to what I was already going through. It was not the cause of my tragedy in life but one that caused a big damage to what was left. All the misery and pain I was accustomed to did not deter the life of luxuries, fun, alcohol, and sex. All I was deep inside was a very sad human.

I stopped focusing on the gambling addiction worries and acknowledged that it had played an important part in giving me strength on my way to exile. I reminded myself that "it is human nature to pick on what's on the surface and make it the cause, while the real cause of distraction lies deep within." At that particular point, I saw the greatest light—"there is nothing to be ashamed of." The whole world seemed to have opened up. One big problem called gambling died at the end of that thought.

My life was unfolding fast and every time it was less scary than the last time. The hospital had provided me with time to reflect back on all the ugly and beautiful things there are. It had allowed me the time to exercise my mental capacity in a positive way, had allowed me to exercise strategies that would help me cope when by chance I had ended up among those in the society I perceived as normal.

I had moved in an igloo style home that I co-owned with my ex-husband. I had come to stay here occasionally visiting him especially when the kids were with him. This time the occasion was different I had nowhere to go and have noone to turn to.

When I had left Napier, it was an extraordinary ward nine emergency flashing lights. I had not been able to go back and sort my belongings out. The last time I had been let to go from the hospital, I made an attempt to bring back my stuff. I only lasted a night and had to be flown out from Hastings hospital by Air Ambulance. Another spectacular event that was out of space, but I was in it.

When I had realized I will never be well enough to go and collect my stuff from Napier, I contacted my ex-fiancé. Tim arranged for the removal of my furniture, and he was to come and visit at the same time. During our relationship, he had gotten a job that required him to get a blood test. I had remembered being worried about he having contracted my illness. Immediately after we got engaged, we stopped using condom. I don't know how to express what it was to spend four years worrying that you are going to be the cause of death of a man you love. The day his result came I was relieved but wondered how he could have been negative. The time he came to visit accompanying my stuff, I was a very different person. I had engaged on looking for a cure to a better life. What I was required to do was what I had thought I will never be able to. Talking about who I am where my disease was concerned was never going to happen. When my ex-fiance had come to visit me in Auckland I took the opportunity to tell him what was wrong with me—only, I did not tell him the the real trueth. He was devastated for me. I did ask him to goand check himself and that gave me one percent of one hundred million of the cure I had thought I needed when he had called me of his negative result.

I had managed to put a few furnishings in place with ex-fiancée's help. One of the things I found and took a second look was a book bought by Tim the Irishman. As I looked at it, something rang a bell about the book and where my life was at. Among the madness of trying to find who I was, writing about my life was now a priority before I kicked the proverbial bucket. I organized my few books, mainly diaries from over the years, on top of a built-in bookshelf. I placed Tim the Irishman's book on top of all the other books.

The top part of the igloo was a large circle shaped area aired with porthole windows. I had set the bed in the middle of the room with the headboard facing the steep wooden stairs that led down into a kitchen dining area.

Down in the kitchen was a skylight window. The kitchen had also porthole windows that looked back into a small backyard. A door lead from the kitchen into a cave-shaped space, and inside was a small toilet, another cave for a shower, and a small corner that could just fit a washing machine. The entire place was built out of concrete, and my ex-husband had told me it was built by the previous owner, a swimming pool builder.

Despite the shape I was in, I loved this unusual place. I had liked the wooden-framed window in the bedroom room. From this window I had a view of a golf club which surrounded two-thirds of the igloo settings. One other view the igloo featured was at night. I could see the Auckland City Sky Tower. Toward the direction of the City Tower was the Auckland Hospital, which was a comforting view.

When my ex-fiancée had left, I felt all the guilt I had felt lifted away when he had called informing me of his wellness. Few weeks later, I had encountered an unusual circumstance. I had been exercising in my room. I used a cool down method that I had read in a yoga book. I had tried this method that required some kind of mind meditation. On doing so I found myself remembering my homeland. I had not talked or thought of my homeland for years. I was saddened how I had gotten so lost to the extent of abandoning my family. The memories of who I was were getting clearer with every event.

I finally got time to skim the book Tim had given me in the short period I had stayed there. I was preparing to write something, something about my life and something that required Tim's gifted book.

I read a passage that said, "The easiest story to write is when you are writing about things that happened to you or someone you know." I had skimmed most chapters looking for a precise understanding. And that phrase was good enough. All I needed was the courage to ignore the reasons I had lived like someone else for that long.

I had been sitting against the headboard, looking straight out to the window in the direction of the city. My whole vision fell back to a room that seemed to take all the pain away and give hope and courage—a room in ward nine of which I had stood still day in, day out mentally visiting places over and over again. Sometimes in the middle of the night I could only hear the noise of those who could not take the pain anymore.

I looked at the bedside drawer where I kept my pen and a diary. I picked them up and placed them on my lap. For a while I did not know why I was holding these two items. Occasionally, time had frozen on me where I had found myself to have stopped. It was obvious that I was too sick to write but all the same too tired to sleep. I had been sleeping for the last few months and still slept most hours of the day. Suddenly, I remembered what I had intended to put on paper. My doctors had tried their best and had kept me in the hospital just in case. I knew I was running out of time. The story of my life had to be told at least to my family.

Then, my life was so complicated and I can only describe it as "the movie in the making." I had no idea how this movie was going to end up. My main focus was to stay alive. Just being alive felt like the part I was playing. And something very scary happened, if crazy can get any crazier. From that stage onward I realized I had no choice but to stop and think. I was no longer dreaming. I was being given a second chance to learn the meaning of life.

Like a cool breeze entering my body, I saw were it all began. The strange dreams that I was accustomed to at a very early age appeared. I haven't thought about dreams for as long as I had lived in New Zealand till a few weeks earlier. A quantum leap is what happened. I leaped back in time and there was the beginning of writing. For the whole night I wrote about the trip from Zimbabwe to Gisborne. I must have dozed off for a while, for when I woke up I was still holding the pen in my hand and the diary had dropped neatly on my lap. My eyes were sticky with tears and my brain had just been frozen to let it rest. I picked the pen up and continued to write. This happened all night and into the daylight; when I had decided to stop for a meal I couldn't. My brain kept remembering more and more events. Things that I had never thought about or never let them hound me flowed in my thoughts, and my hands were busy writing. The night went by and the morning came. I felt my eyes becoming too heavy to open. I have been crying all night. Everything I was remembering was so sad that tears were pouring out of my eyes uncontrollably. I hadn't realized to what extent my life had been a horror story till that day.

My daughter walked in, into that mess and did not know what to think. She comforted me while she joined me in the crying. She was on the phone to my hospital doctor within seconds. "I don't know what is wrong with my mom, but I think she needed to see you right away," she spoke. With that my doctor instructed I go to the hospital to my ward. At the hospital I told him that nothing other than my existing condition was hurting me. "I think I need to see a psychologist. I am going mad." These were the actual words I said to my doctor. Lucky there were always psychologists. I was to see one right away, particularly the one that had shown interest in working with people with AIDS.

In her practice room, she got me talking. I told her my life story and nothing else, and for the first time, I had told another person my life story in full. At the end of it, I asked, "Do you think I am mad, doctor?" "No you just need to grieve," she replied. Back to my ward I was given seductive pills to help me sleep and discharged the next day after My doctor had come back on duty.

As for my doctor, I don't think he ever knew that the writing of my life story had triggered another disease, as I did not disclose this event. The psychologist had recommended grieving. "But how?" I had thought, allowing the hot lump on my heart to break. The next couple of days, I was well enough to go home where I carried on writing. I was writing everything I remembered about my life and had no I idea about my life tomorrow as tomorrow was never to come.

I knew I was tired of trying to manipulate my own life. I knew I did not like the person I had lived. I knew people did not know the real Sophie. In spite of all this, most people I had met wanted to know where I got my strength from? That had nothing to do with strength as far as I was concerned. They didn't know that I was trying to reach out, deep inside my soul I was yelling, "can somebody hear me!" Instead that did not paint a picture of a crying person. If I was myself I could have preached the words of 'Do not judge the book by it's cover'.

After weeks of writing that felt like a lifetime, a one-way street suggestion began to take over. I had discovered that part of my illness was caused by the person I had become. The people that mattered the most were worried about me, yet they would be careless about the diagnosis. As a thought either way I was lost. As fragile as I had become, I did find laughing with myself. "How long can anyone live like someone else, an hour, a week, or a year?" I was thinking that if given a second chance, I could not live like someone else ever again.

With each day that passed, I could only walk back in time and come to a realization that this was going to be a long and lonely battle. The good thing was there was a hint of relief wherever an effort was made. Whoever said "round in circles" would have had experienced something. I bought into this theory when I thought and analyzed my life story over and over. Only one day I said, "I can see what happened" and "I could see what could happen."

A family day is when we have had a meeting that reflects or plans the next year in our house. One of the findings was to face up to my kids. I had asked my kids to come over this particular day. When my kids came over, I immediately spoke in a low voice. The voice my children knew was only used when the substance was very important. I was glad because my body was not nervous. I was used to turn a situation on and off in the last decade, so I began. "You know the mother you have always known, which is me. Everything you know about me is very much me." That was me talking to my kids. The day I found out about my illness, my kids were in primary school. *This time they were not kids. They had grown into gorgeous brother and sister.* It was fourteen years to this day. I told my kids about a very large piece of me that I felt was removed, the reason I did not bring the babies home when I had come back from Australia, and how I was left to figure out how I should survive. I spoke about how I felt and why it had to be a secret.

I felt as if I had just said I am not your real mother. I had just told my children that I had lived with the HIV virus since they were four and six years of age. I told them about places we had lived and the stories within the family they grew up. I apologized for making those decisions. The room went very quiet except for my voice. Both my kids were looking down. I had no idea what they were hearing me say. I looked around the room and felt the proudest mother alive loved by the most two beautiful people in the whole world. My children cried for the longest I have ever seen them. They wept and wept. We all cried.

I thought, "Poor kids, do they have to be born in a vicious circle like this?" I wanted them to stop crying and laugh with me. That is how we've always been. "Hey, don't cry I am not dead yet." Somehow I have always tickled my kids' ambits with words. We laughed as we all saw the fun side of life.

Peace of mind is what I felt from nails to toes, even thigh muscles, and felt a sense of being and being counted for. And I felt like a mother who was a protector—I could not accept any other title. Later that night alone in the igloo, I wept and felt tears washing away the pain.

There was a time I used to wish I was a government's project; life could have been much more, easier. I was told, "You are the first case in this country." It was not a bad wish. I wished if that was the case of new diseases, someone might take some interest in people like me; at least I could have had a better way of coping with life and maybe have had a better understanding, in order to keep up with my health. A year went by, another, then another. I did not hear from anyone. Someone felt if they did that I might feel like they were praising me. Or maybe I wasn't the first black person they forget to add that one. I disregard the reason was, stopped wishing for their rescure and created a life for me. A dangerous life as I see it mostly the danger was inevitable, alcohol, cigarettes sleepless nights and the rest that went with that lifestyle. As no one was watching me I was killing myself faster than the fast lane I was living in. The tears that hurt so much poured endlessly and at times I looked in the mirror hoping to see blood pouring out, but soon even the tears dried out.

IN THE HAZE OF LIFE

*g*od had answered my prayers. I was feeling much better within. Every day became a day to cherish. One Mother's Day, I found myself talking to a friend about what I had been up to. A friend had suggested that. It would be nice to be mothers away from the kids that afternoon. We decided on going for a drive as far as we can get but ended up by Muriwai Beach in Waitakere, west of Auckland. While sharing our lives, I realized how lucky I was to have been blessed with the gift of children. I could not have participated in such a set up if I was a single person. While exchanging the past few years' events, I had the opportunity to recall the last few years I had been a patient. Being a patient had been easy to discuss openly because my friend had learned a lot about my secret life in the last few months.

All I had been hoping for was change. What I wanted to happen or not happen, I had explained. I just wanted to get better, which was asking for too much from what I had already been given. My wish was for changes in choices, to be loved for who I was, not to be ashamed of who I was, to experience life, and be thankful. All this sounded like if I had to beg, I would be hearing answers like, "a beggar is not a chooser." I could not remember when I had last looked over my shoulder or the feeling of something bad hovering above my head. The worst of times had been my health without that extra stress.

I had not been in hospital for some time except on occasions, when I had been admitted for a day or two, then home again. I had no idea how many times I had been in and out of hospitals. It was better this way than living there. There were improvements in my well-being. I was aware that there was nothing the hospital could do for me as they had tried everything. I had been to and from the hospital many times and each time I had left with one or two added types of medicines. I had those many types of antibiotics, above all the viral repression tablets that I had been put on. I was a moving pharmacy. I did not want to think of how much of all those I was taking a day, let alone how long that was going to go on. Life was getting better, so I dosed myself with the hope that one of them might give me a chance to live longer. At this stage, life for me was better than I could remember.

Most times when others were predicting their emotions based on full moon, I was busy creating an environment that was not influenced by society. I felt I was being able to create and set standards for myself. Humans can never be satisfied. Especially in my case, how long am I asking for now? The last time I asked God for lenience I asked him to give me fourteen years. He granted me that and somehow I could feel him saying, "Next time have faith in me and let me do my job." At this point, I was not to dwell on praying for more miracles but work for a better future. Thanks to my mother who in her prayers had said, "God helps those who help themselves." I knew I was taking medicine to help the person I was looking for.

With very little effort, the spirit of life was coming alive. I was sharing all this with my friend who thought her marital problems were bigger than the one I was telling her. My friend thought I was luckier than her, and I could not have had a secret life, she had commented. Everyone thinks the same, I had thought. "I don't know how you do it," she had said. If she only knew that even I, did not know how anything happens around me only knew what was inside me. This conversation is probably the most memorable as I was talking about things that I had never shared except the physocologist at the hospital. I was beggining to appreciate the human race's ability to care, especially the few I had learned to trust and accepting empathy. I felt strongly that I had the ability to think constructively and felt proud of myself. At the end of our day, I promised to give her a copy of my story that I had started writing. "It's only what happened to me," I told her. But she was keen to read it.

When she had read it, she returned it with the following massage: 30/09/03

> "Sophie, I have said these words before: You are truly amazing and a
> hidden secret to a lot of people's survival living with AIDS. I feel that
> I am blessed to have come to know you and I am even blessed that you
> even trusted me enough to share so much of your life with me. My life
> is chaotic but please let me help you to be heard. It's what you want, and
> I want you to be heard so that our children may learn from this. These
> lessons are more than what I could teach. I love you so."
> Sissy Eve.

Between days, weeks, and months, I had only remembered good days because I made use of them to spend time with my family, going to rugby matches, gardening, and painting my house. Writing about my life was always a way of venting out loud to invisible audience. I did what I could do weather permitting and a combination of how my body felt. Life seemed to have been teaching me a lesson, and I was one that would not sit and listen. I was the one that refused the normal theories of life. Somehow I had learnt to negotiate or agree to disagree if that had made me feel better.

At war with myself was one of those things I spend time doing? I had no idea how I got time to even think of my behaviors. I found myself thinking, "Some habits are hard to change." One thing that I had not figured out in all this was a habit that I have, whether it is a disease or not. Despite the illness I live with, I am the biggest flirt in the world. I was aware that, this kind of behavior in a person like me is considered abnormal. I had questioned this and considered changing, but like the virus I live with, I could not shake it off. In between days I was feeling good I had polished myself like a female peacock, behave like one something I had loved. Learning to live the new life I had been daydreaming as what normal people accepts me was scary. It felt like what I was looking for needed to be a public announcement. Yet my behavior would be judged if I was to be in a public arena. Well, I had to carry on as all the other behaviors I had accumulated come to surface. Somehow I contued to justify why these behavious are in me.

I had begun to see a new me emerging without any announcement to the world. I got out every day when I could. I could hardly do much, but the body had been battered. No one did notice the difference in my appearance I could notice. I was frail and fragile. I knew under all the makeup I wore painted was a very sad and confused person. A lot had happened, and I had been on my wobbling feet for a while. The brain was never at peace, always busy but calm. "Just because I am sick does not mean I should look it." My mother had a bible of life saving ways of thinking methods I call, 'A must to have in your list of things to remember'. "What disguise what's in a home is the roof," she had said. Even at this, age my parents's way of parenting came to the rescure.

I felt like I was sent to a different galaxy, where it was a nonstop driving traffic system. If I had stopped, I would have caused accidents. A galaxy were thinking about what I just did, what happened, what I am going to do and what is going to happen might cause a break down. So I kept moving until nature decided when I should stop, how, and what I will be doing. Since 1989, my life had been a shadow. I could not recall daily events, even yearly ones.

Remembering daily events was now an achievement. When I was sharing changes in my life with my friend on this day, I could feel the spirits encouraging me not to be scared. I was discovering and learning what stages of my life I did and did not live. "All most all stages" I fell on unsatisfactory box. If this sounds crazy, what isn't considering where I am coming from. Memories are like good dreams you want to remember. I was learning that good memory guarantees a smile on every person's face and the bonuses are those memorable experiences. I had remembered who I was and where I had been. What I was remembering was not the greatest but turned to be a life well earned, I felt. Recalling life as it was and explaining the next stage sounded like mission impossible. I wonder why my friend had a worried look in her face. Going back to find myself was a topic I believed she thought would be impossible. One thing I know she thought was that I was crazy to think I needed to change the way things were; she did not think there was anything wrong with being Sophie. How bizarre is that. No one ever guessed who I was, and now, loved ones were probably scared for what I might become.

The exciting part of my life is that they were so many doors of issues that were being opened that I had always thought they can only be discussed by intelligent people. I had told my friend as we walked back to the car, "Do not get me wrong when I sometimes describe intelligent people as smarter than anyone else. I do measure how they became to be perceived." As a joke referring to these intelligent people, I had said to my friend, "Do you know what rabbits thinks when they are caught by the law-hunters?"

She said, "No."

"Rabbits don't think at all. They feel humiliated when they get served as a salad to the eagles," I explained, and she thought that was funny. I did learn to distinguish jokes and insults in my own daily contact and some jokes should not be taken lightly.

"Is that a true story, Sophie?" my friend had asked as we sat at the edge of the beach.

"I have more stories to tell if you want," I said, and we both laughed hysterically. A whole lot of other things I had not discussed or acknowledged came out on that Mother's Day. Something in me was very different. I was not feeling the ground but just a breeze of relief in the days and weeks that followed.

The best was yet to come. I was feeling it. That was a change when I had always expected something nasty following me. I had felt that maybe the next Mother's Day was going to be better than the one I had spent with my dear friend. Around the month of August that year, one afternoon I got myself ready to go for a coffee with my daughter. She had called me the previous day and asked if I would like a day out and a talk. I picked my darling daughter, whom I called Barbie. I had always called my daughter by her pet name, maybe because I did not want her to be a grown up, maybe because I knew I will never have a baby again; so she remained my baby. Faith is one thing that I noticed I was trying very hard to restore in my heart. When I had been diagnosed with the deadly disease, my daughter was only four. This was the reason I had asked God for fourteen years. At this very same day, my daughter was five months away from turning twenty.

Smile was coming from the heart, through my eyes and ears; just about everything that was Sophie was smiling. I did not need to explain why I was smiling. My daughter was next to me in the front. She sat with her gaze fixed straight ahead as if she was the one driving. She began to speak in a very calm voice as if she had been rehearsing. "Mamma, you are going to be a grandmother."

"How did that happen?" I said, without taking my eyes off the road.

"What do you mean how did that happen?" she threw the question back at me. We found those few sentences funny and we both laughed. I glanced at my daughter while driving and noticed she was crying. With one hand, I stroked her leg and wiped the tears with my finger. I pulled the car over to a stop. "Don't cry, Barbie. You know babies know everything. If the baby thinks it is not wanted that, is what the baby becomes. So we just have to start loving this baby from now onward." As she wiped tears off her face, she said in the saddest voice I have ever heard, "I know what you are going through, Mamma, and I understand." I understood too what she was going through, and only this time I was the mother and a grandparent-to-be. What do I do? What was I going to do?

The whole day I was telling anyone—the service station attendant when buying petrol, the bank teller when withdrawing money—that I was going to be a grandmother. I told the whole world. Was I in a state of shock or excitement? I think both. When everything had sunk in that I was going to be a grandmother, my body did not feel like I would be around if things carry on the way they were. "If I don't make it, how is my daughter going to cope with a baby alone," I told myself that many times. "Don't think like that," the other voice butted in. When I managed to push that thought away, another thought would say, "Please, Lord, don't let anything happen to the baby. I won't know what to explain to my daughter, and I don't think I will have any strength." Every time this happened to me, I found myself hanging on a piece of very fine cotton. I felt like an old tired lady dragging a very heavy load. I was losing my strength by the minute. My daughter was tired and possibly the saddest girl on earth, but the strength in her was a paradox. She did not know I knew she had the same fear. She touched me, fed me, and incubated over me just like the pregnancy she was carrying.

By the middle of December 2003, I had brought to the attention of my doctor that the pills were killing me, and I had preferred to stop them. He had disputed the fatality of doing so. Stopping my medications would result in worsening my condition, and there were no other treatments left to try. Even when I requested more tests on the newly found disease that he said was causing the lymphoid and pain, it was declined. I understood that "yes" it was a waste of time and money, but I was not well; I had to try. At this stage, I was on morphine and worried that I might have been addicted to painkillers. But that's all my doctor could do. I had a lot to pray for, somehow at this time I had learnt to be happy with the moment. Realized that this time it's my call or else I was not to see my grandchild being born, I got the courage to stop all my medicines. My doctor was not amused. I still had to beat the addiction of Prendisone, a very addictive drug I had been on for nearly three years. I became very weak as a result of all this. My skin had changed into a darker dry shade. I had bright red eyes; heavy bleeding from my mouth and constipation was my nickname. The fighting machine I normally am could not think only hope remained. What I had been day dreaming about finding a cure was not going to happen in the state I had become. Automatically, I shut down as if I expected the miracle to have a loud voice. Not this time, no miracle, not even a whisper—just silence.

In spite of all this, my daughter ignored everything she felt in her body and comforted me. I was worried and scared for her as I could not even pretend to smile or eat. I think her father and brother were scared for us both. They could see the way we just clung to each other, and I knew they felt powerless.

Earlier in the year, I had been watching Super Fourteen rugby at a bar near my house. It's a passion of mine. If I can crawl to a game I usually did. This is one thing that I inherited by becoming a Kiwi. I had always watched rugby since I arrived in New Zealand, and now I am addicted to watching all the international games. The best of which is to be a prominent supporter of a province; in this case I belonged to the CRUSADERS. I still do support the big guns, The All Blacks. The Hurricanes were playing THE CRUSADERS on this particular night. On the night, I met a Wellington supporter, and it was obvious we were oppositions. X was his name and lived not far from my house. After the game, we realized we liked the same things. One thing led to the other.

X said I was amazing. With those words, he turned my whole world upside down. I had not thought all the imaginary practice I was daydreaming in hospital would happen. He was the first person who had had a crush on me since I had been back from Napier. With all his charm, I did not know what to say, but eventually said, "How so if I tell you who I am?"

"Try me," he replied.

"I am not a normal woman," I said, but that did not make sense even to my ears. After clearing my voice several times, as if I did not know the story I should be telling, I got to the point. "X, I am not fit to be loved as I am dying." He looked at me for a long time as if he was studying the meaning of what I had said. "I am not a normal woman," I repeated, tears pouring down. I was lying on my back facing the ceiling. He was lying next to me listening to every word I was saying. He leaned forward, kissed my tears with a "shhhhh!" He held me for long until I could not make any sound. Amazing grace, I had a date to watch the Blues vs CHIEFS that night. When I had found out I was going to be a grandmother, I could not wait for X to come home to hear the news. About my boyfriend, I don't know how he could have loved someone that needed twenty-four-hour care. Something that I can't explain I had realized that or assuming I am not contagious after four year relationship. How is it no one can't get the virus off me? How can I discuss this finding openly if I am not supposed to have a sex life?

When I was near death in hospital, I wished I had turned into an alien as I had always believed I was one of them, and that did not happen. With this man, I see it as the gift of nature to keep one important aspect of life working. Maybe it is because in my life love was and always will be on top of my priorities, if I can share it. My family felt like that thin cotton I was hanging off; that's how I described life at this stage. Christmas Day was the same as the last two previous ones. Cook a big feed and let the spirit above us have sorrow if they really cared about my family, a short visit to the toilet for a short emotional cry was part of a Christmas celebration as long as I come out smiling. Christmas day had been one of the many occasions where my family got together like a peaceful protest, and we had always won our protest by the end of the day.

In January, my daughter went into labor. My boyfriend took us to hospital just before midnight. A walking zombie is what I was. Probably the midwife thought I was half drunk. The state I was in was a sight of life gone wrong. I passed out for a couple of hours, and my daughter was trying to get me to be admitted on the other side of the hospital but knew I would not take that. The next day at 12:40 p.m., my grandson arrived, without a word to explain the feeling. It was one part for the emergency shift well accomplished. I managed to be with my daughter and watched the little man being born and that is one memory I would never forget. I was there to watch my first grandchild get dressed, weighed, and spend his first couple of hours with him, despite that I was a shivering weed in a flowing river. That evening I went home. I wanted to come back and see my little man, but instead, I passed out in the short nap I had intended to take, and had a very, very long sleep.

If I had ever known what life could be for me, there is a lot I should have prepared for. A kitty box for occasions like this, a suitable home for a welcome home to a very special person. After all, all these years I had thought I had something for my children when I die, but that was to prove me wrong. I had prepared as much as I could in five months. Only if I was myself the last sixteen years, I thought. "Never mind all that. What I can do about it?" That was me talking to myself, trying to preserve any little energy I had. And it was time to visit my grandson that morning. I named him Kingston Jayantha Farai. Kingston is his uncle's middle name, Jayantha is his granddad's middle name, and Farai is my native language, which meant joy. I personally liked the sound of Farai; the meaning of it is what my grandchild is to us, joy. Kingston is that one other gift God withheld from me for that many years. Another reason to be thankful. Being able to write my life story and events like these happening at the same time gave me the pleasure to say this. "I am very lucky to see one of this book's pages forming itself. I had thought I will not find enough people to dedicate this book to, but now I have."

It is the things that I did not think about that filled the time in between. I always had something going on. Now a grandmother I was focusing on the new man on hand. Even the pain seemed bearable. Only the mind wanted to believe that I was getting better, but as the result of stopping the treatment, I went straight to worse. I went straight to worse as my doctor had predicted. I was going down steadily anywhere. As it turned out, it was a decision well earned. Going down fast was scarier than ever before; maybe it was the first time I was scared of dying. During the time my daughter had been to university, a friend of hers had suggested a Chinese doctor that he had been seeing. She told me of this doctor and handed me the card. I had thought my situation was about having incurable diseases and flag her efforts. Fortunately, I had kept the card on my fridge. Shortly after my grandson was born, I had been admitted but sent home the next day. The Doctor had suggested I go to hospice home. My daughter called the Chinese doctor in fear of what she understood of the hospice facilities. "Your spleen is in bad shape," he had said. I was given some Chinese herbs, and a week later I was back on my feet with a bit of appetite and a little energy. I visited my hospital doctor who was quite frankly shocked to see me walking. I let him know I had taken alternative medicines, and that I feel caused some improvements. Usually, after every visit, he had sent a message to my GP. This day saying my spleen has recovered and its good news. I had already questioned if my doctors knew about the spleen and decided not to tell him about the Chinese doctor's comments. "Well, what is new? Maybe they think I would not understand if they say 'your spleen is damaged and you may die.'" In the past, some situation like this could have sent me packing. Seeing the Chinese doctor was a credit I will always owe my daughter. Pictures are sometimes a perfect way to express meanings. I have a picture in my head that is so vivid but courageous. I wish others can see it through my writing because on this particular period, how was this exit going to be easier for my family especially with a new baby? Secretly, I thought God was being so cruel to my family. Barbie, my daughter, had become a mother of two, and she was trying very hard not to cry.

Its times like these that I had stop doing things I was doing like writing about myself or put aside what my intentions were and focus on the family. I had felt this so many times. I did not expect much in life because the chances were always something nasty would be waiting around the corner. That could not have been less than accurate. Few weeks after I had seen the Chinese doctor, when I had just thought I was getting better, something called neuropathy peripheral, a nerve condition, struck. This condition would paralyze my middle spine down to my feet in a matter of seconds. This gradually happened several times a day. So regularly it happened even in supermarkets as though I had fits. In the shower the electricity like would shoot through my nerves reaching my feet in seconds and I would drop to the floor. When this had happened while in the shower, my twenty two-year-old son who had moved in to help with what ever it was I nedded would come to the rescue. Its one of those moments I had not imagined would happen between mother and son. Without a notice, this nerve condition became a skin condition. With the disappearing of the nerve attacks, I felt itchy—so itchy that I had to be admitted to hospital. My doctor treated this condition casually and said they knew what was causing it. They meant the HIV virus was causing this, so no treatment.

Nine months had gone by so itchy I could not concentrate on anything except sitting and scratching day and night. I was more of a monkey, except a monkey seems to accept it and its not irritating mentally. Again and again I was admitted to the hospital. On the other hand my grandchild was growing in all this. I knew I had to try and get rid of this itch or I was going to lose my mind. I had started to think of all things unimaginable to my beliefs, only I couldn't. Taking my own life was the scariest thought I had anticipated due to the itchy so far; at the same time I was feeling alive inside. And again my daughter went to see a South African doctor of whom she thought would try and get her a skin specialist. The specialist gave me body lotion and a five-day course of tablets, and I was on my feet within a day, after nine months of suffering. So how do I not find in my heart the gift I was given by God? He gave me children for a reason. Being able to socialize and play with my grandson was all I was asking, but I got more than that. I got better and happier in a matter of days. So it was, "Where was I again?"

The best part of all this period was the time I was trying to figure out what living was. I bumped my head a couple of times and tripped over occasionally, but hey, the walk in the haze finally showed a bright light at the far end of the tunnel. It had been months, and I had no control over what my life was going to be the next day, even the next hours. I had listened to my body for signs of, you may be able to do your washing or washing and vacuum your house. So I did learn to appreciate people around me and let them look after me. For the first time I did not feel the shame of losing my dignity but accept and appreciate this act as a normal human act when one is in need. For the first time in my life, I opened up to another human being and let her view inside my world.

"My life is full of shit." I had said this to my friend Angie. Angie was my best friend, the first person I called a friend in Auckland. We met in a night club the first time I went out clubbing. She had a smile that will open a jammed door. I fell in love with her at first sight. We were very much alike, full of life and loved life. Like me, Angie had been married and also Angie had traveled immensely. I feel bad that our frindship was was one sided in a way. I think Angie enjoyed my company and it would not have matter that I was waiting to die. She had laughed to my jokes that weren't jokes but the only way I knew how to laugh at myself. "How could you insult yourself like that, Sophie?" she had asked, soon after she became the name caller. "Sophie, you are full of shit," which I gladly accepted; I was.

If anyone had come to know my life within, someone could have accidentally noticed the scary things in it. These were scary things that did not have pity even if I was not doing anything. Things were happening around me as if that was part of a normal life. I believed I had a spell that was to be removed when all the methods of pain had been inflicted. "You can never get used to pain" was a statement I had to dismiss. I learn pain can be endured when life is perceived as more precious. I was accepting pain as part of fighting for the life campaign. Opening up to another human being is something I had been longing for a very long time. I have been battered physically and emotionally, and all I was now seeing was glimpse of hope.

Coming Out of the Closet

One day as I walked the corridors of my ex-husband's house, I caught a reflection of myself in the mirror. We had been having a farewell lunch as my ex-husband was traveling overseas. Occasionally, we had a get-together with the kids to share lunch or dinner. From the time I and my husband seperated we had get together for any occassion regardless how little it was. For me and him we knew why this was important to the kids. Most importantly we had enjoyed each other's company.

Nevertheless, something in me questioned curiously what it was? I moved the top half of my body backward to see what had caught my eye. It must have been the image of myself. I could see nothing other than the wall opposite. I stared in the mirror for a couple of more minutes, touching my face, and still not see what had caught my eye. That day after lunch I left for my house, which was not far away from his, the house we had built years earlier. Another healing day, I had thought, when the memory of the reflection had stayed with me.

Later that evening, when I had gotten home, I read my 2001 diary, remembering the conversation I had had with Tim the Irishman. It was nearly four years since I had met him. "Look into the mirror. If you can't see anything, keep looking," he had said. I had been touched deeply by this Irishman's words and the circumstance in which we had met. How could I forget the time I felt that something very large was going to happen. I was tired, fragile, and frightened. When I met Tim the Irishman, I had forgotten what I was living for. I believe people passed words of wisdom to others when they had found a purpose for living. My parents use to say, "Listen when someone is offering an advice. The chances are that they have lived it, and they know what they are talking about." I find myself reminding me of that saying. I believe my journey to exile began the very next day as Tim's words of wisdom opened another channel of memories.

The next day I cut my dreaded hair off that I had grown for seven years. The hair was the only thing I could pick up on from seeing a reflection of myself at my ex-husband's place the previous day. All night I had felt as if the hair was carrying a curse from every path I have been. Sure enough I did not miss it. I felt lifted and clean. The weeks that followed I scanned my reflection in the mirror in search of a connection to the soul inside the human image that stood in front of me. So the search for "I don't know what I am looking for in the mirror" continued.

My health was improving slowly but surely. Strangely, I began to fight with boredom. I was feeling energetic mainly from my brain that would get so excited with each discovery. I felt I had gotten my life back enough to be doing something. One aspect of life I had chosen was to keep the spirit of survival alive. "I am not invalid," I told myself. Invalid is one of the many new words I did learn, from having given a status in the social welfare. I was feeling confident. "I have got a lot to give were always my favorite words that comforted me." I had been thinking how I had been at the mercy of all the horrors over and over again. How I have not been able to organize my thoughts and prioritize my responsibility for so long. Now that I was feeling that I had been given the ability to scrutinize inside the person I had become and the virus I live with, what do I do? "Please Lord, help me! How do I become a better person?" I had prayed.

"Coming out of the closet" was a whisper from the silent voice, the voice that listened to me, talked to me, comforted when in pain, and held my hand when I was lost. I had responded to situations absolutely absentmindedly as a result of this. "Coming out of the closet—how easy is that and how?" Aha, my mind rushed to the hospital room where I had walked to and from a million times and back again to this crossroad. How can I help myself? What is the cure? And all I did was craving for a public announcement. I had been crying to be heard. With that I did not need to research the meaning of the message the secret voice had told me. "My life is about the disease I live with, and the disease I live with shadowed the person I was supposed to be. There was a great reinforcement in my physical and mental being as the result of practicing telling my story." I realize that what I was practicing could be the act of coming out of the closet. With the little effort I had felt that I was being rewarded with peace of mind, and every day that passed, my health clearly showed improvement.

In hospital I had learnt what I was required to do in order to get complete peace of mind, so I went on a quest a little canning but I am no jornalist. I assume that my experiences have been experienced by many people with or without an illness. Due to what I have experienced, these events are some of the things I had time to reflect on.

> Once upon a time, I gambled my life day and night and had my heart torn into pieces every second of the day.
> Once upon a time, I drank every night and experience headaches every morning.
> Once upon a time, I smoked thirty cigarettes a day and smelt like a rotten fish.
> Once upon a time, I slept with men who just wanted someone to offload on, and I wanted someone to hold me, then woke up feeling like shit.
> Once upon a time, I spent every second worried if my appearance matches the expectation of the society I lived in.

Above all I lived with a very dark secret that scared me and sent me driving in fast lanes, only I was lucky not to crash.

"Dark closets indeed," I had found myself agreeing loud. In hospital I had visualized myself in those situations and thought, "How are other people able to turn their lives just like that?" Coming out of the closet for me is all the above as all those did surface on a daily basis.

My interpretations of living with HIV virus are a sense of deep loss, fear, loneliness, and isolation. I was presented with the unknown and that filled me with fearing for my life. At the time I was diagnosed of the condition "acquired immune deficiency syndrome" I did not know what that meant. What I do know is that my mind left the room upon hearing the first word the rest echoed. The mind left the room immediately and run to see how hard it was going to home. Who am I going to meet first?

I once lived this moment and this is the reason I feel the need to share with people of all backgrounds about what went through my mind. What is it I want to achieve by telling my experience, and why is it an experience now? There is nothing like experiencing a situation, a fact I learned in the days I was in hospital. At the largest percentage anyone who has lived a situation can lean a great deal more than they realize. Through this experience I was luck inough to ende up in a serious thinking position. In this experience I discovered that positive things can come out of the negative situations.

Pride is a positive attribution to life. I was brought up to understand what that was. But I was never taught the opposite of pride. I had to learn that the opposite of pride is shame. Pride does not compensate shame. These were contributing factors to my suffering. When I felt my dignity being stripped of and replaced with shame, my whole self went into hiding. If I had only then "stopped and thought" who, why, and what I was hiding from. I realized what I had failed to remember. I failed to remember the word humiliation; being humiliated does not kill. I failed to remind myself of the other humiliation I had endured before and survived. It was one requirement I needed in my life to be able to endure shame.

When I woke up to what I now believe was the cause of my misery, I did realize that I was forced to feel shame by people who took the shame upon themselves. The shame they thought would be a bad influence to the society. Quietly walking on the dark side I discovered that we are a society that feeds on influence. I never stop and think of the situation I was trapped in only rushed to create a world of a shamed person. What I had assumed as normal society drove me to a dark lonely island. I had to be near death when I asked, "Why should I be coming back to life for?"

If I could change anything, what is it I had to change? I rode a merry-go-round for hours while in hospital till a nurse, doctor, cleaner, or the coffee/tea guy walked in. Shame had become part of me since the day I was diagnosed as HIV positive. I lost the posture of pride when my babies were murdered; life changed into a heavy load that I had to carry it on my shoulder. While on the merry-go-round, it became clear that the shame had something to do with my hopeless situation.

In recent times, doctors have changed their conduct with the HIV sufferers. "You are HIV positive," sounds a little gentle. In those days the actual wording was "You have AIDS." As I was diagnosed during this time, there was not much information. My understanding is to date when diagnosed early with the virus you can still live a normal life provided you understand the crucial key to stay healthy. On the other hand this means at some stage your body may not be able to fight some other infections that might attack the body compared to someone who does not have the virus. I was going to die within eighteen months; if lucky, I would live for five years.

The most pain I suffered was fear. I had run from nothing but the images of the killer virus and the horrors of what was coming. While running away from the virus, I was looking over my shoulders wherever I was. For uncountable times, I did ask myself if I was a criminal? I had wanted to know why I felt like one. A small situation like breaking my leg. I could not sleep. Anything that I had accepted as normal life I had put them under the radar of suspicion. I became paranoid due to these changes. Paranoia was a symptom of the fear and consequently it became an illness. I was lucky enough to recognize that while in hospital.

When I had accepted the virus I lived with, understood what was the cause of what I had been feeling, I felt better much better. "This is another requirement, a part of the puzzle to a better being," I had acknowledged.

I strongly felt that the virus needed exposure in order to sustain good health.

I had found freedom and wanted the right to cherish the person I had lived. When I discover the cause of all the pain, I decided I was going back to face the day that changed my life in order to continue living the way life should have been. To do that I had to accept the condition my body was in and made it part of my life. I have talked about how society did play a great roll in my life since I was diagnosed. In Sex Love Life and HIV chapters, I have talked about how influences cause distraction if it's not the right influence in society, what silence can cause to those who are suffering, and how those influences can be caught in it, if we do not stop and think. It was too late for me. I had been suffering for years, but luckily I found the way.

The turn of events suggested that I had been blessed. My life had been sad, so sad I did not know the difference between day and night, so sad I could not separate good from evil. So sad that I did not understand what I was living for. Somehow what I thought every person should live for was fading away. I was living in a lonely jungle; even the jungle was starting to show gaps. All the trees, grass, and shrubs I had been sheltered by, began to give way and every time closer to the scariest and darkest part of my life. What I was afraid of is what was next.

It took thirteen years before I was on the ground. I lay in a hospital bed when all the things I had wished for did not appear. I believed I was an alien; at times I had wished I had transformed into an alien in an instance. I had meditated for a minute also forcing the power of an alien to transform me. I hoped I would transform into a dragon or some very strong creature, so I could tell everyone how I was feeling. Well, that did not happen. I continue falling in a deep dark hole. Inside the dark hole was tranquility that seemed to promise a good night's sleep. But that did not happen; instead the doctors were trying very hard to bring him back to life.

When weeks and months had passed by, I could only say I had a lot more to worry about if what I felt was real. I was feeling that I might not die, as I looked through my hospital window. At that particular moment, I saw the light. I saw the real world and the influences the disease had on the entire world.

It was the day I found out about my illness. How could I forget what happened on this day? No not this day. I do not ever want to forget. Initially it was not the disease that scared the skin out of me. It was who was going to be my friend. And who was I going to tell. That was then. Today, twenty-three years later, nothing had changed. People are still faced with the same issue. I experienced loneliness and isolation from only that point of view. That is where I felt the need for change as this was the first point of shame. The society became the biggest jungle; now I realized what I was required to do. I had to change the way I was thinking, the way I had seen things, and the way I lived. The battles I was fighting were everywhere—my neighbor, the school teachers, my workmates, even my children, the list went on. It was about the society we lived in that scared me. When I had felt the society I lived in could care less about what happened to my babies or how I feel. How was I to live and participate among them? I felt pain was inflicted beyond the words and what more could they have done to me to fear them. At that moment I saw the light and felt I had a break through toward the cure I was looking for.

I was no longer going to trip over the virus. I live with the minute I had acquired the requirements to deal with the problem. My experiences had concluded that there is a myth to everything. In hospital, I was used to telling nurses I was positive. I did this on purpose as part of my duties. If I were to get a second chance, that's how I was going to claim my place even if it meant that changing my name to HIV. I wanted to see if I could actually say it. All nurses had read my files before they attended to me; somehow discussing my situation to them opened a better communication channel. One day, I caught a taxi from town back to my hospital room. I did not look very well; I don't know if the Indian taxi driver noticed. He asked me where I lived. I told him, "In the hospital. I am an HIV patient." The taxi driver said, "OK." I was surprised by the tone of his voice. And I realized I can say this to anyone; it's not so bad after all. Encounters like these gave me the strength and new hopes that I can live in this society as long as I have the attitude.

Being really lonely is something I did not talk about because I do not know how I can paint loneliness in a picture. I think when a person is happy, they will never be lonely. Before I thought that far, I had to accept the change in my health and how I could live with this illness without stress, to accept and find ways of living with this virus, not fighting it. Fighting it had only resulted in stress and misery, I had recalled. People I saw in my everyday life were the reason I was so scared to come out and flourish. What they think is based on what I think as well, I had found out. People I have met since I chose to live again are not so frightened but surprised that they are people like me that exists.

For questions like "Do you know how you got it?" I used to feel like saying "What the f—does that matter now? Help me!" But I could not ignore that question because many times I have been asked, I had actually tried to think how I got it. And fortunately I have experienced it all and witnessed the power of ignorance and the distraction it causes. I don't want that for my children and anyone's children and the generation that follows. How I got it is no useful information. From where I stand it's about taking action and control of my life.

I don't know anyone who is friendless at all,. In a population of four million that we are in New Zealand they will always be four people that will be my friends, is the way I supported my actions. In situations where people have conversations, I believed they found something in common and they might be trying to explore that. And sometimes they make an effort to meet again. Many a times this has happened to me in public places like a pub, supermarket, even in the doctor's surgery where some people have told me all about their misfortunes. These persons were not making it up, and they were at a point where they don't care who they tell in the world. They just want to talk to someone. When does it make a difference in how dramatic my story and theirs? In what circumstances the stories should be told. For years I did not think I had the right to participate but to listen and smile or offer sympathetic gestures. With all the courage I had acquired I did finally find a way to participate or say I was learning to see an opportunity to practice what I had to do, and from nowhere, I had also shared my secret.

Some of these times I had found myself responding to their heartbroken story by saying, "Well, it cannot be as bad as living with death." This kind of talk sounded quite scary to my ears as I was not used to talk about death loudly. Amazingly those I have spoken to wanted to know what I meant. There are people out there that have problems smaller than mine, and they have the right to offload them on me. I met people that had listened to my problem without saying, "Hang on, but your problems are not acceptable." I lived with the virus for over twenty years, I had said many a times. On some occasions I have heard some say, "You look pretty good." That had put a smile on my face as I had not asked if they meant I looked pretty good for someone with AIDS or as a woman. Such a peaceful feeling, I have experienced it.

Body shock is a situation I created the day I became a shamed person. Body shock is caused by deprivation due to being isolated. In the first days of my isolation, I did not understand why I felt like I don't have a shadow anymore. I had felt like a shell, more like being naked in public, and that feeling made me feel unworthy around other people. I had not liked to stand out in public, even dressing up like I had always done. All that I sensed was being an outcast of the society. As times went by, my personality had changed dramatically.

What had happened to the body as a whole? I had stopped laughing; instead I cried all the time I had spent hiding away. I am generally a chatter box and all of a sudden I had nothing to say, or shall I say, I felt I had nothing sensible to say. Every speech I was to give had to be customized or was not exactly the way it happened. I thought about the same subject over and over. I only discovered that body shock can be avoided during my unresearched theories. They are things that could have helped if I had prior knowledge of what was to come. As a result of this finding, I do not visit my doctor for the body shock symptoms. All I had to do is change that.

Love is such a strong word to talk about. How is love part of my well-being? If so, could removing love out of my life have caused body shock? For many reasons I had wanted to know what love is. I talked about this to the based on my experience on LOVE SEX AIDS AND LIFE. Long before my ordeal I knew I knew that I was a loving person. And I believed I had carried love with me through out such a lonely path. While in the middle of healing and fighting to live again, love issues crept in my head every time. I thought about how I had lived like someone else. As much as I rate myself as a good lover and a lovable person, this department was never in existence. Now I have the knowledge of what is true love and intend to live and experience it. Subsequently love can be only found if I am honest with people around me not ignoring the fact that I had to find myself first.

Things I did learn are that I had to be whole inside out to be able to live as part of a loving society. "That" maybe not up to me if the society I live in does not want to know. What I had to accept is that the disease I live with is part of me. Therefore, I will acknowledge it in my wildest dreams. We are not dead till declared dead, I believe. Till then I will love and as a believer there is someone out there that will love me for who I am. When these thoughts first enter my mind, it was a joke as the result of who would want to love a sick person. When I tripped over the ignorance issues I had been the victim of, I realized that sometimes the human brain is our own scare crow.

With regard to the immune syndrome and their theories, there are those theories outlined in this chapter that may have given me the chance to live longer. Our immune system, I believe, respond better in a positive environment. Yet when it comes to the virus, it comes with the entire negative, a stigma that scares people who live with the virus and cause destruction in life. Shame cause diversity, loneliness causes mental trauma, and mental trauma becomes the illness. I believe that our immune system finds it difficult to fight mental illness if not the only. If life is the one we don't give a though review like a home work, it is obvious this lead us to live for influences as the engine of life. I had to learn that living life through magazine, books and Ophra shows is not enough if the reason is not to soul guard ourselves. I believe that in positive thinking even when I unnoticeably lived like someone else I still emeted living a happy life only it was not fulfilling. How was I going to live among the community if i did not pretended to be like them? Something had to happen when all of a sudden I was afraid of the people I lived with. I did not realize I was creating stress in my life. It should not have been that way if we had perceived ourselves as a caring community.

I was taking a lot of medicines and still do. With all due respect to these medicines, I believe coming out of the closet is one nonmodern medicine I was looking for, and I never thought I will have to travel forty years back looking for where the pain was. I unbuttoned every piece of me to find which one does what, the things I had said I could not play doctor on myself. I had the opportunity to understand how power hunters save the rabbit to the eagles. How the rabbit can be humiliated by being saved as a salad. In my own opinion I have leant that ruling others cannot be simplified or taken lightly. In a modern world, we ought to learn to be rulers of our own lives. Above all through coming out of the closet, I had a quiet time to grieve my babies, and I know they did hear my prayers. To the world, my prayer of wisdom is this: "If only I knew what I know now."

THE LOVE, SEX, HIV, AND LIFE CYCLE

*L*ife, how many of us have been given the opportunity to look at our lives from as far as we can remember? Maybe from the time we were still clinging at our mother's back. And how many of us have assigned ourselves to look at the meaning of life or a meaningful way to live life? Or is there a meaning to life or a meaningful way to live life? How is that when given the assignment? In the previous chapters I have talked about who I am and where I am coming from. In all that I was living, eating, sleeping, working, making babies, but what is that I said about living? Nothing at all because I only talked about what everyone else would say when talking about their life, in other words how they live it. Immediately, I found a problem within. If what I have said about my life already constitutes living and the meaning of life, then I could not move on to the next day. Saved by the bell, something beyond the ordinary happened.

If living is life, what is life? Beyond all the things I have known and learnt, this is one question I never thought I will have to deal with. I had never thought there is a need to ask this question at all. In spite of everything it never occurred to me that I might have to ask this question as part of searching for a cure. As it happened I had to come up with my own definition, (my definition is based on my personal experiences) maybe the only way toward change in my own life if I should clearly illustrate what is and the meaning of life to myself.

Life is only life if lived and shared with the same species; let me explain why. I had to imagine sharing life with dogs on an isolated island. "Which is exactly the way I felt I lived for twenty-three years. I could teach them a lot and they could have understood me. If a crisis should have risen, such as dinosaurs" coming to the island, telling them could have been easy, but would they have understood the danger of not taking action? Dogs cannot stop and think and do not have the ability to plan ahead to prevent danger. This scenario would have to take its toll. My experience of growing up in vast, cruel, and changing world has taught me a lot. From my own experience I am convinced that it could not have happened if interaction, ideas and watching out for one another was part of the society I lived in. With principal attitude today, I feel strongly that it is my duty to share what I have seen as part of the species I belong. I am positive that someone will one day stop and think.

Living as someone else for that many years, I lived a normal life. Many a people would write me off from the thought of me having love affairs, having sex, and even walking into lives without their permission. If that is the case, I should not claim to have lived a normal life. Love and sex is very much part of our lives. Regardless of what this is about, humans do interact on every level. It is this natural act of human life that I suffered the most. Guilt was probably what I was suffering from. Why did I have to feel guilty? What is it I did that made me the guilty one? I just had to remember that I lived with a virus that is not accepted. People around us do not talk about sex; therefore, I learnt a great deal about behavior, attitude, and beliefs also, about love in general. Like dogs in the isolated island, most of us have never stopped and thought what is love and how does this relate to sex. Why should we think about it? It is supposed to be a natural thing to do after all. When I heard this quote in my own mind, I realized that, that was the reason I was feeling guilty. Something that is not natural had visited my world and the world I lived in wanted me removed.

With the guilty conscience that overwhelmed my worth, I began to analyze everything I said or did. The most intriguing part is every time I had tried to express love, I had said, "I love you." My heart would jump, if I had said this to a lover. Fun is that I have said "I love you" to a lot of lovers. On the other hand, I could not even attempt to say I love you to my children. I could only whisper it in my heart. The question any one would like to ask is why whisper. I had the same question too: why do I love them and what is the meaning of love? These questions were not given a thought as the thought could have resulted in an assignment, which in those days was going to be impossible, so the mind did shut down. What is meant when "I love you" words are spoken? Has the word love got a definition? Try to define this word in no relation to life. This is the story about my journey, analyze this, a task I never volunteer for, but forced to look into, and try to make a difference to others so I believe.

During my struggle to understand the world I lived in, and the person I had become. I came to realize how foolish I was to think I can love someone and be loved the same way. The day my marriage disintegrated I did not realize I could still love nor have the ability to love regarding the situation I was in. For years, I did not fall in love or give it a thought. I was busy creating a new life for my kids and me. Life was changing by the day; I did not realize this. I had new friends, new places to go, new home, even new clothes. Kids were growing and my duties were becoming less stressful. It is this time I tramped on the love track unexpectedly. Love is a word and a game with no rules but purely intriguing. It is this segment of my life that made me look inside the love triangle and the meanings behind it all.

My love life was full of fun, fear, danger, and abuse. When I began scrolling back, through my love path, I learnt that there are categories that have been designed to interact to form life. And love is within those categories, if not the most important. Therefore, those categories should have an honest and meaningful character in order to function. Life is the main stream and all we need is the oxygen. Love can be lived only when all information about life is gathered. In all those years I lived believing I understood what life was about. When I was thinking about love, I knew I had it in me, although never trying to analyze what it was. When I went looking for my soul, one path I could not avoid looking at was the relationships I had with the opposite sex. I had a problem with sex consciously, but that was one thing I could not live without. Unconsciously, that was one way I was going to receive the other kind of love. And a whole lot of issues came to surface. One of those issues included sex and the disease I lived with. It is then I saw the danger of ignorance of influence in this subject. It is then I realize the story of my life should be told as it happened, so I will have the opportunity to share my concern on love, sex, aids and life. Shame, I had to overcome shame if I had to find a meaningful life.

Being in love is maybe the most complicated kind of love. When you love someone normally. You feel the need to be loved back. The need to be loved back depends on the level of emotions shared. When I mirror at day one, when we all have met that one special person that make our hearts jump by just thinking about him/her. The chemistry in our eyes, the sensational feeling that hardens our tits, at that particular moment there is an isolation of life. Nothing has entered our thoughts only dominated by love. This other person became part of our life in a flash. A happy long lasting love life depends on the other party, if he/she feels the same explosions of feelings just by a touch of a thought. This is what I meant by it all depend on level of emotions if this is how I feel when he/she touches me, what next? Needn't I have to say more. This first day physical attraction and where it leads to is what makes love as to the meaning and feeling complicating.

Four out of five people has experience the feeling I have describe above at some stage and we all call this love. Yet two out of five have had sex outside the love fever (one off stands) how does that work? (This statistics was provided by many of my friends and associates) We believe sex is part of love; yet sex is triggered by what we feel as love, when the physical side of our life takes over. It's unimaginable to those who have sex whenever they want, to think that they are people who never have sex. A common course of not having sex is a strong belief and some degree of disability. Sex is a chemical in our body that causes lust and therefore this is the reason sex is not, a basis of love nor a major part of loving someone. I don't know what those who never experience sex thinks on this subject. Maybe it is true that, "you never miss what you don't know" I am not going into chemistry now as you probably know by now that my education was done and over with in fourteen seconds. I understand sex is a chemical that is easily triggered by visualizing, sounds and even smells. Bearing in mind about all this; sex has no meaning when defining love. I am saying this because once you have sex you are fine, all the visuals and the smells disappear just like that. People can have sex without love for the other party, yet it is supposed to be a result of loving someone. Did I say suppose, when the chemical of lust takes over the conscious mind, the unconscious mind then translates this as love? The nature of this love way before humans recreated themselves had a different approach to it. In the Stone Age sex had nothing to do with love so as love had nothing to do with sex? Both love and sex had a specific purpose in life and never was meant to be associated. (Some African marriages demonstrate this point of view and today some Indians culture still indorse this kind of marriage)

As I have experienced a long single life with no one to love, my body constantly reminded me that there was something still active in me. And it was not only me, because if it was only me, then I will never ever have had sex out of not being in love. Sex is a category of love that is part of life. This is where I have chosen to begin my concern. There are people like me single and having sex. "Yes" sex has now been proven to be used for a loving gesture also for having fun and most times means of acceptance. I was once having sex for the purpose of feeling loved and to be accepted even if the person did not know that's all I longed.

If you haven't agree with me yet about sex and love's theories well try and understand where the subject of LOVE, SEX, HIV AND LIFE is heading. Sex is a segment of love. Love is part of life since the beginning of nature. Life is the main stream the most precious, just being alive. I have been thinking about how HIV relates to all this. I did not have to go researching on this subject I have firsthand experience. Un like a cold that has existed for generations, (HIV) did not exist forty years ago, I believe that it's a virus that has evolve in humans bodies through our ignorance of ignoring what is supposed to be sacred. So where do we place this virus today? If it was not part of nature is it now?

HIV virus is going to be part of our lives if we all decide to ignore it. HIV is a virus contracted through body fluid, (don't take my word that's what my doctor told me) fluids that is able to be passed to another person and able to live and grow in them. This form of transaction of the virus can be through blood transfusion; injection or even passed on to an unborn child. So how does HIV relate to love sex and life in our society today? Sex is a proven most commonly way of its growing numbers. I am talking about if HIV is part of my life, now known as, "living with the virus" how does this influence my love and sex life. Does sex chemistry disappear the minute you get the virus? I have not yet heard of this from my doctor. The stories and happenings that I have heard and encountered, has not yet suggest this theory. So if HIV has qualified in the main stream why is it a secret? Or is it the sex that is a secret? I have spoken about categories designed to interact with each other to form life (the main stream). What do we do, when a situation as destructive and deadly automatically qualifies in our main stream?

Dear Lord should I start talking about what we all don't want to hear. The main stream has changed from those our ancestors had swum in. Our ancestors lived in islands that they share with their own and no dinosaurs where going to attack their dogs or they were to perish in the ocean. The Stone Age is truly history; we live in a galaxy filled with people from other islands. I am talking about people like me I call "people who live among us" regardless of where they are from. People who turn up on our island boarders like me that grew up in fourteen seconds and overnight I was turned into an invisible dinosaur.

Sex is the most performed activity that humans perform millions of times a day. The nature of this virus has qualified in the category of sex, because it cannot be cured, more and more people are living with it. Therefore as I see it will soon be a category of life for everyone. If there are people out there that have outlived the darkest days when there was no medicine. Today the term person with AIDS has almost diminished replaced with people living with HIV. I am happy with the new term are you? Although the common cause of spreading is sex. The virus its self does not create a device to change your sex libido. If sex is seen as a result of any kind of love people are not going to stop having sex, because HIV virus does not stop nor make people lose the feeling of love, How I lived is a good example of what I am trying to illustrate.

Influence is created, therefore it can be fixed. HIV influenced my whole entire life not just my sex life. People have leant to ignore this; the big picture is the influence of silence. Now it's me who have a problem, It's me who is the sinner and the criminal. Is it because I did not master the art of removing the feeling of love in order to stop having sex? Having the virus in my life was very frightening, more frightening than a bullet two seconds away from reaching my heart. If we look around us, there are people who are clearly frightened. It's not a laughing matter. With all the wisdom I have been blessed with, I still struggle to find the right words to explain to the world. I do remember going to get medications not long ago from the outpatient clinic; there I had been so disturbed. I had thought, "Why is the government thinking putting all the black men in prison is going to solve the problem?" Most black men those found to have a sexual relation while affected were being paraded on television as a means to safeguard New Zealanders. To see the sad part of this is if you had gone to the outpatient clinic where the black man comes in chained to the prison warden. Some of them were clearly ill. And we were all happy these people should be punished. I am positive, this kind of influence to ignore need changing.

It is human nature to forget. People forget to think in advance. I had now realized maybe it is essential. I tried to justify everything I did one way or another. I was thinking it's too big a task to tackle or how big is my voice. My outlook and understanding of the meaning of life was not in line with what I know now regarding love and sex. Now I know I cannot love or expect to be loved as long as I choose to participate in this society where the subject of sex, love, and life is not being revaluated to date. The mainstream has an added category that is fatal. If to love is part of life,

I believe to create a meaningful love life is when both parties are able to make choices.

I have so much love to give, I had thought. The challenges I face are these: how I am going to understand the world of the disease I live in so I can help those who are suffering with me? Would I ever find a way some day for a practical solution to all this so I can receive pure love? During my soul searching, I found out why I could not receive a meaningful love from anyone because no one knew me. There comes the fact of life, the meaning of love, the nature of sex, and the virus I live with. It is all clear in my mind this might not work for me because I have to start the trend. "My name is HIV—what's yours?" From the statistics there is someone out there who might be thinking the same way. But how do I know if I don't give them the choice? This has so far happened and men think I am crazy as a result of influence. I did not think I could ever tell anyone even in the dark that I am HIV positive. No one says such a thing when she knows the guy she is looking at give her that love fever. It must be a joke. Is this a joke if you hear it happened to your friend in a different place with a different person? There is hope to start respect and be truthful to ourselves and others. Ignorance kills faster than a car crash.

Would you think I am crazy if I ask you this question? Would you please give me your honest opinion? And here is mine. (E-mail me. Thank you.) How would you respond if you take a girl/boy home because you have visualized something that triggers lust? He/she says I live with the HIV virus; this is at your place. Do you throw her/him out, go and vomit in the toilet, or stop and think? If you stop and think you have been given a choice. "Given a choice" came from a man I encountered with in my crazy days of my life. He looked straight in my eyes and said, "Thanks for giving me a choice." In reality what kind of person do you think this guy is? A psychopath, a snob, a street kid, bisexual, rich man, maybe is a poor one. A guy I will never forget because he showed me that the worlds I think exist do exist. There was and still is that stigma that only gay men get it. At least they don't have to live like someone else. They have a choice. If you get to know your partner there is another side that influences more honest and enjoyable love everyone has in them. After this incident I thought, "If I choose to talk about me louder, I may be able to receive pure love and sex working together." I used to fantasize about this, but I do not anymore my efforts has paid off. Hopefully, this method will unchain HIV sufferers and their victims. Many of these victims are the influence of silence. No one wants to address the existence of this virus; I am back to the stigma and the distracion that the virus is causing. People prefer to say one day, "I don't know how I got it." And in a flash their lives have been turned upside down overnight. It is the society we live in that has created the people who live among us. I was one of those people (people with no choices, the outcast of a perfect society). Nature will remain and influence will destroy or have the power to build. I believe I have been shown the other side of us, and only I want to share with everyone without shame. If you should find reading about how people have sex, where, and when, this is not what it is about, This is about sex as part of human nature, HIV virus a disease that has qualified in our main stream, and maybe about time we start thinking why am I taking off my pants if my plans for tomorrow does not involve him/her.

My life has been a university, except I did not get a degree. I have so much to do as from now. If it's tidying up, it is like tidying a very large old deserted hot dusty island. There are some shocking stories I can tell from those I have nothing to do with. My story is being lived by someone else. Someone is living with shame and guilt; on the other hand someone is feeling he/she has been victimized. People are still scared today, and they are trying to bring normality to their lives. Only that it is creating what I am concerned about. People have to try and find means of accepting HIV virus in their homes as part of life you can talk about. I have been given a second chance to put things right and get on with my life. But I feel I cannot just accept a second chance without a purpose in life.

I was searching for where the horrors of my life began. Instead, I had to travel back in time to when I was a sperm to put the pieces together. While

111

searching one spot that I could not rub off or brush down even ignore was the virus I live with. Every undesired spot I spotted somehow was easy to cover up or ignore. I could not even foresee how it was going to be a completed puzzle. Tiding up my sex life in relation to HIV is the only way I can deal with the spot that I cannot ignore. Michael Jackson said, "If we all try our best to change the world, we will change the world." I believe, as long as people love, they will lust. Does this mean I believe people are going to accept people with HIV to the right of sex? Yes, I do and those without the right to choose to have choices without alienating each other, only if I accept my role. It has proven possible. I am practicing what I had thought was impossible and too frightened to practice. That I fell is the only way to be complete another reason is, this has proved to be the cure I have been looking for twenty-four years.

HIV has been the reason for the loss of my children, the reason for living a horrible lonely life, not able to perform well in parenting duties, for lost time and opportunities, plus a whole lot more. The pain I suffered of not understanding the choices that was made for me. I never thought I will say, "I am HIV positive to anyone even blindfolded in the dark and in another world. I never could talk about my babies to anyone in case they might ask how did I lose them. I could not tell a soul a reason for visiting a doctor. I could not tell a lover that, something is eating me when we are alone in bed. But now I can, and I think the time is nearing to unveil the birth and death of my children. People are much the same out there. If I was encouraged to accept this some years ago, I think this could have saved me a great deal of pain.

We live in a world of misery and pain. It seems like no one cares; with all that people forget that their lives are like a stream, when it rains all dirt from miles pours into it. People are so buried in their daily problems, money, addictions, family breakage, and illnesses. These people do not pay attention to inner self. Broken souls do not guard our well-being; we just get worse. It's what doctors refer to as "immune defense, the lower they get the higher risk of getting infections." That is what HIV virus is; so will be tomorrow's generations. And as one of the people who lives with the virus, I have seen too much to realize that they are people living with pain equivalent maybe to mine. The difference is they think they have many years to live. Many years to live is where their pain differs from mine.

These people have reached a point in life that they would not want to hear something like, "You have five years to live." Time to fix their problems is all what they think about. Sometimes they don't know which problem they have to fix first. I will rephrase this; most of them they don't even know what the problem is. One thing they haven't stopped is living. When I use words like these, I automatically travel back in time, when the doctors said I had only five years to live if that. At twenty-six, I had two little people to take care of. I was a migrant from another continent; one thing I could not afford was to stop living. Life is a stream, and it comes with all its categories, and where it ends is how we perceive it. Somehow, I have seen them all. I have also seen the influenced once.

The influenced ones. They have everything going for them: a handful of good friends, sustainable jobs, desirable wives, kids, university students, steady girl/boyfriends, excellent health, good family, and family homes. These people are on the move: the café life style, pub scene, night clubbing, traveling and parties. The influenced people live life to its true meaning; they are the fortunate ones. Knowledge is something we all think come from a text book. If that is all to a better life, then I am afraid we need to think again. If it is OK to separate ourselves from those we perceive as unfortunate, I feel there are those who are fortunate that might need to stop and think seriously. What I am trying to say is unless we start putting signs like "for the fortunate ones only," there are no rules on how we meet and associate. One thing that no one can change, that I for one can has seen is, life stream and all its categories. I have met them all. Fortunately, I was in it as part of a hidden secret that no one wants to talk about. Across the board, these groups of people have one thing in common—they all agree on "choices in life."

I am very lucky because I feel equipped emotionally. In some part of writing about my life, I referred myself as I was. I was talking from a time frame point of view; at that time that's what I was feeling. When I accidentally tramped on my soul, at a blink of a thought that felt so strong my life took this turn. I could not find a better way to express what I think is a problem that is not far away from everyone's doorstep. Then writing became the only way I could start the process of healing. That became the beginning to a road to freedom; whatever the outcome, I will not live like someone else.

I believe in what I had seen and what I can predict. For the first time, I had time to stop and think and for the first time I put myself first and fear last. In February 2002, I thought there must be a way. I had to find where it all went so wrong. How I could change everything and start to live again. That is how much I was hallucinating as this was to be a first-of-a-kind treatment. I lay in a hospital bed for six months but did not know what I was waiting for. It was obvious this was my last place to call home. Someone had to bail me out with a second chance. The immune syndrome had set in; my body could not cope anymore. The mainstream (life) was in distress; I had to be stopped. The anguish, stress, depression, and pain all took their part. Hospital is like the sea where all the loads from the streams of lives end up. In my case, I called this "the survivor at the end of a search of a sunken ship." What would you do if you have been in this ship I lived in? Do you go back to your usual routine? If you know what I know, the thought of living the past will take all my energy. There must be a better life and a better way to communicate as a society, I am convinced.

My theory to what I call conspiracy by the law-makers is based on what happened in my life, and I as a mother went along with it, and my children became part of what I accepted, the children of silence. With that I have allowed and opened a door for them to be victims of influence. Yet they should have had an upper hand on education about sex and sexually transmitted diseases. Lawmakers get paid to make laws or change where necessary not Huber us when it suits their needs.

I have decided to stop playing the lawmakers' victim and stop them from victimizing our children with their influence of silence. If they only know life cannot function without the truth, my life is one I will never wish on my worst enemy, but I did accept it for twenty years. We are not dogs in an isolated island; let's stop and think. If law can be made, then it can be changed according to our changing lives. I believe we can destroy the ignorance caused by influences and protect the stream of life. Start talking about protecting our island in advance, together as humans. The meaning of life can only to be understood when all the information about life is gathered.

Tomorrow, a Distant Dream

There must be something special about tomorrow. For me today was about what I could do if I could. When I began writing my life story it was a journal for clarity; it was a memorandum for my next generation to understand how they got here. Tomorrow was never to come; the only important thing on my list of things to do was a short story to my kids before I had kicked the proverbial bucket. Some of the pages where written in between scary situations and some when writing was the only thing that I had energy for. By the time I felt I had said enough I was somewhat a different human being from the one I had lived all my life. The experience I acquired over the years from cultural upbringing, motherhood, migration, being oppressed not forgetting being imprisoned by the virus that needed a home to live—I had acknowledged all that and still felt there was something that contributed to the person I had become.

When I thought I had found a recipe to cure myself, it was just madness. I was talking to myself through writing. I did not have a manual except the memories of the path I had traveled. As I was so lost, I needed to understand how I got that far and how it all started. "To hell with that," I had thought, that was not important anymore. What was important was to look for reality and what's normal. My prayers were about tomorrow. What tomorrow will bring me if given a second chance?

Second chance was well and truly waving some hints. That, I felt blessed for. I was still learning a lot and everything I had learnt so far was worth every effort I invested. In the haze of my life was a turning point, and I had thought I knew where to go by then. Because of the status my body was in, I felt like a cat in a sack. I was trying to get out, and that, that one thing I never knew what it was, came back and said, "Chill out, Sophie, I will let you go when you are ready." Finding me depended on what happened to me. As far as I was concerned, I was ready, and tomorrow was never for me.

I decided to jump the gun and leap into tomorrow. There was one more puzzle of my life I need so much to understand. The search began. To me it was an enormous effort to find if there was anyone out there who can help. With no experience, I had no idea who was an expert; something in me said, "Lawyers." I had thought they can help me with the process. The only place I suspected I could find some answers was the one I was scared of, and that was the lawmakers' office, in particular the ministry of health and the immigration department. I hold my head high, breathe in, and make my first phone call to a lawyer. The lawyer described my case as old, the second one, as an issue they don't deal with. I did not give up hope. I went to number three, then number four. By this time, I was questioning my own skills. What was the right and intelligent way I should be presenting my story? I was getting tired of being asked to repeat myself over and over again and at the end of each appointment I had a three-hundred-dollar bill to pay. Something triggered my mind one day after I had spent hours asking myself if all this was normal. Or should I even consider asking the government department of such a thing. What if they did me a favor? Nothing could stop me. I was ready to confront my past, but physically I was very tired. "Are you on anti-depression medications or have you been seeing a psychologist?" All lawyers had ended up with that question. I assumed that these common questions indicate that my story was unbelievable, and only someone with some kind of mental illness can come up with such a performance of imagination.

Eventually, I found a lawyer who I thought was helpful. He introduced me to another lawyer he had said had the knowledge of human rights. I was confident on this one as I had not even thought that I had any right. I felt I might have to explain the intelligent way this time. I was to receive a call from the other lawyers, so the next day a lady contacted me and arranged to meet at my home. After she had asked all she wanted to know, she took my written short documented story and said she will read it and make comments. Before she had left, she informed me of her husband who she said was the lawyer, and as his secretary, she had come on his behalf. Weeks later, I got a letter in the mail stating her husband had read her notes on what I was straggling with and recommended counseling through social welfare. She also suggested that I was suffering from sexual deprivation. Those comments really hurt. I thought, "Did she even listen to what I was telling her?" As for counseling I had been with qualified professional ones, private and through hospitals. One thing this lady did not know after I replied politely, asking she send all my papers back and thanks but no thank you, was I am one person that could have given the counseling on sex deprivation in her life. I did feel sorry for her and wondered who she was working for and what gave her the right to insult another human in need. Mind you, I only believed I was in the category of humans in need. Every person or organization I approached treated me as if I was out of my mind and too far with it for them to help. "Maybe it's all in my head," I did wonder many times while trying to ignore the fact that I had spent thousands trying to find if I had contracted a mental illness at the same time. Some experts did politely say, "It's an old story. The law puts time limit on complaints."

"This is not a complaining issue. I am looking for help," I had thought.

When I started writing my life story, I was desperately looking for a means that was not medicine. Fun that all the methods I came up with to archive results required one other person, so I had thought. I had thought there must someone in this society who could help me. At the point my health was not an issue; only my mind kept clicking. All what I had to do was to be happy with what nature was providing. I was feeling I may have a second chance, a second chance I had no idea what it was for.

When I began writing my story, I was miserable, lost, desperate, and above all angry. I thought I knew who I was angry with. I also assumed that even if I demand answers I was never going to get them. I could not fully accept that what I was feeling about answers was OK. I wanted so much to understand what happened to me and my family. In the first chapter of this story, I can hear the storm of anger in my voice. But I kept writing to a point that some of the persons I perceive as oppressors of my childhood were brought up to surface. Not only the ones I know of, but how the world is shaped and influenced by the same blood that craves for power over others. Chapter after chapter I kept writing until the anger and the frustration began to fade away, so as the pain and the disease I live with eased off. When that happened, I put the pen and paper under my bed.

I knew I talked to myself a lot. Within the inside thoughts I had, there was always another voice that would come up with comments. This time its comments where "Send them the copy of your story. You have nothing to lose." I instantly knew who it was I was to send the copy to. "What do I do? These are the people I am scared off. Why on earth would I do that for?" That was me talking to myself. One day I got the urge to send the copy to the Prime Minister Helen Clark hoping they will see how I made an effort to help myself. How writing my life story saved my life and prevented my children from becoming orphans. How selling a book can take me out of the poverty that now looms over my family. I was begging for help to publish my story that was. In reality I was scared to start with. I need the answers from you.

Nevertheless, I was delighted when I received a reply from the prime minister's office that read,

> *"Thank you for sharing your story with us and the courage to talk about such misfortune, ThePrime Minister has asked me to refer your letter to the right directions that will help with your request. Yours, Honorable Judith Tizard, on behalf of the Prime minister."*

I was stocked, over the moon more like it. I knew of this this name Judith Tizard she is a very powerful woman. Surely, she was going to help me. It had taken a long time to get replies the first time. This time I followed up on which charity Judith Tizard had consulted with.

I head from the charity the prime minister's right-hand lady had recommended after I had to chase them. They were not sure if the right-hand lady had contacted them, could vaguely remember the conversation. But any way the lady did recall the conversation from the Beehive and couldn't remember who she spoke to.

For weeks I was sent to so and so, then to some organization. Finally I was in the hands of the department of a charity for misfortunate people. In a phone interview, I was asked if I was mentally ill or was taking medication as their charity only worked with such people. I ended the conversation rudely by refusing to give them my personal details. That action was caused by being scared of feeding myself to the lion's mouth. Nevertheless, I got a laugh out of that. I laughed so much that I ended up with sore ribs; another joke I thought. I thought I know I am mad and why do I think any normal person would even consider me normal. Whatever they perceived me as, I got to understand what so-and-so interns had to say, "Sorry, we cannot help."

From that moment I had a feeling that my companion's voice was never to come back, and this time I felt all alone. What was I to do? "Forget all that, Sophie, and start again," I had told myself. I thought to myself what would the little voice say if it was to come back, "Get off your butt and get a job. You are in control of your life now." That was hard, very hard. What kind of job would I apply for? I had lost confidence in the working marketplace. I had not worked for anyone for as long as I can remember. "Nonsense," I was talking to myself, "you do not need any of that. Start looking." The second phone call I made was in response to an advertisement that said, "Do you enjoy hard work? Would you like to learn while you earn?" With that interview, the next day I was working. I became a room attendant in an inner city hotel.

There were times I watched television programs on people with similar issues and how they found themselves again. Somehow most stories had concluded that when people get the opportunity to expose what they feel, and the courage to say, "Yes it happened to me and this is where I ended up." It was simple in my mind. Just because what happened to me was overlooked does not mean the damage was never greater. Or is it that what I am feeling is rather normal and do not require experts' help? I focused on daily events rather than finding information that I felt might not have been recorded. As for tomorrow, that was to remain a distant dream.

I was feeling worthy more than I thought I was worth, even in the eyes of my creator. Anything new I was very much welcoming with anticipation. It will take some years to score another miracle in a hat like this. I had say this with a huge smile on my face.

They maybe some things we all would prefer never to remember in life. As it turned out I got to remember every little moment I had lived. Surprise, surprise, there are millions of behaviors and abilities that I still hang on to. Some of all these I had used them to manipulate or distract situations purposely in order to survive. At the same time, I knew what I was doing. I knew these abilities could be used for good purposes and work all the same.

Thinking had become my brain's playground. I was now convinced that I had been frozen for a long time. So I had a very long time to grow and learn. Living the best I could did bring my life to a new level. I found where the pain was; with that I learnt to cherish my illness. My illness had a better place to live if it was a human being. I had a sense of spiritual survival. I was feeling that I had conquered the devil that was on me and had defeated the evil that fed from my misery.

I had acquired a better understanding about who I was, and I wanted to explore more about that. As a result of all that, I came to feel and hear with my heart, not with my head. Once I read an article that stated, "Without a soul it will be very difficult to survive."

I was relating to the subject of the importance of the soul and the body. I was never able to survive anything from this time if I had to lose sight of my soul again. This time I could feel my soul, the reason I was now being able to pitch in the world I was scared of.

At some stage the physical being I was never was in existence, till the day I said, "Now I get it." What I meant was what I had discovered about being a being. Being a being is nothing short of that world that exist among us all. For me, those many years I lived like someone else I was looking for a visible world that had disappeared. One afternoon while having a fag outside my house, an airy feeling overwhelmed me, and I felt so much at peace. So at peace that I realized it was not because of the state of my body, which I had not felt for a while. Possibly a week or so I had not felt any aching, but did not notice the change. Something lifted out of my heart, and I felt happier. So happy that the instant I remembered the day, I lost my shadow. When I had stood up and looked across my neighbor's place, I felt normal.

I had been racing for a better tomorrow just to be part of the society. Something I lost the day I found out about my illness. Over time the need to be approved by the society diminished. In this society once you are out of the team, you are out. For years I had played the game alone and lonely. I was working on how I can become part of the society and seek forgiveness. Even that was scary with my brain constantly in the thinking playground, I felt not the end. There was more, much more to come and waited to find what that was.

Growing Up in Fourteen Seconds

The vicious winds blow and blow
The trees shook and shook
A black fertile seed dropped
Dropped deep in a fertile land
It began to grow fast
It grew faster and faster
As fast as it could

In fourteen seconds it was larger than large
In twenty one seconds it produced seedlings
Out of its roots came the seedlings
Seedlings like a cactus holding onto the stem
Black as black was its color

The winds from the west blew and blew
The trees shook and trembled and trembled
In twenty-six seconds the black tree got sucked
Sucked in by the tsunami
A tsunami from the west

The tsunami gently glides back west
The black tree sailed and sailed
Sailed along to be left on an island
Battered but standing
Standing proudly by its seedlings

In twenty-ninth second the judgment day
In twenty-six seconds the black tree was judged
What is a tsunami, what is a tsunami?
The black tree cried and cried
In twenty-nine seconds death was upon
For thou tsunami is nature
For thou tsunami is nature

The black tree the black tree
Nature whispered
By the fortieth second
Nature did prevailed judgments

I am glad to get to talk about where I was coming from. I was born in Rhodesia in the province of Murewa in 1963. I was named Christina after my grandmother's younger sister who delivered me. My grandmother Sophia whose duty was to deliver new family members was on holiday when I was born. When she had returned four months later, she protested that I have to be renamed after her. My grandmother was a fortune-teller, and she had apparently foreseen my mother's productive activities, and she knew I will be the last girl of the family. With no negotiations at all, I was to be called Sophia and no one was to mention Christina ever again. As my grandmother had predicted, my mother never had another girl. I am one of nine children and the second to last. I am also in the middle of the only two boys my parents could have after a string of girls. It was a disappointing time for my father as he had expected to have a second boy. I grew up to understand the importance of having boys traditionally; I also learnt that my father came home to visit the family as he had always done not because there was a new baby.

I had one grandparent, Sophia, who was my father's mother. My grandmother was the oldest granddaughter of the chief and was a much respected lady. My father was her only son, and she also had two daughters. Traditionally, a lady of her stature had to be honored by naming one child after her. This was not just any grandchild but preferably a grandchild from a son. They also used the stone to the throne traditional system. And I remember when I was growing up, I had the pleasure of living as my grandmother's shadow. I was always treated with respect by village elders as well as all my family. One of such privileges led to mischievous behaviors that led me to finding out my first real name.

My mother was an orphan; apparently, her marriage to my father was arranged by my grandmother through my mother's uncle. As we were growing up, we were occasionally visited by her older sister and brother, but we were never taken to her home province to meet them. Her background was that of a Christian, and the only one in my family. My mother taught us about Christianity more than her background. The only way she had spoken about her childhood was when she was angry and then turn anger into a lesson class. Occasionally, what she did speak off had always left a repeat play in my mind and understood the sadness in it. Things like she slept in sacks as blankets or her brother had to get married at a very young age so he could look after her and her younger brother. I never was told what happened to her parents or whether their death happened in one day. No wonder when it was story time, she rather talked about God. Her childhood was very sad. All I knew about my mother was she was the most dedicated parent. And as a parent now I even think more so.

My father's father was a chief from the eastern highlands of Salisbury called Inyanga. Inyanga was famous for tea and coffee growers. Historically, the tribes of whom my grandfather comes from were traders. The history of my father's tribe is that they originated from Mozambique and fell in love with this fertile part of Zimbabwe as it was known then, way before the first traders came to this part of the world. Way before Cecil John Rhodes claimed to have discovered Zimbabwe and called it Rhodesia. After my grandmother was divorced from my grandfather, she returned to Murewa and that is where my father grew up and had little to do with his father. Even though we never had the opportunity to have a relationship with my father's family, we retained my father's real family name (Mubvumbi) of which a lot of Mubvumbi families exist in Inyanga today. Amazingly, I learnt a lot about my father's background through my mother. I think my mother was very proud of her children's background or she felt it was important for us to know. The only teachings I got about my father's background from my grandmother was when she was complimenting my younger brother Alfred. She always praised how gorgeous he was, and the tall gentle good looks he had, had been from our grandfather. My father worked as a driver for a Safari company most of his life in Salisbury and came home once a month or a three-week Christmas holidays. He was apparently raised by a white man where my grandmother was a housekeeper and a mistress to. Proudly, my mother will tell us how he was only eight when he had started driving. He also did not attend much schooling but learnt most of the written and spoken English language he required with his driving from this white man. As a Safari driver his duties were driving tourists from Rhodesia to South Africa via Botswana, Zambia to Mozambique then back to Rhodesia. After years of this, he retired to a more stationed driving position which was to test new buses. I was about eight when he moved to an office type setting rather than on the road. To me my father was always a visitor mostly welcomed but mysterious.

As a child I did not have many hobbies except I loved swimming in the river, fishing, making dolls from old clothes, and making fishing hooks. My favorite food was anything my mother put on the table. We did not have much variety of foods, the main dish was always maize meal, green vegetables cooked in peanut sauce or garnished with fresh tomatoes and onions. Once in a while, we had meat, especially when my dad comes to visit. All this seems little but when I think of what my village was like, I can only say a paradise that angels visited only at night as they would have had a spectacular view. Houses were at least three to four acres apart and it was a mission to visit neighbours or go play with our cousins. The area surrounding my house was flat and had very few large trees. This provided a distant view of hills in a line to the north. The north had a much fertile soil as they always had better crops and most sold vegetables came from those north villages. When the baboons had their festival, we had had the opportunity to hear them scream, although the hills were visible it was a good half a day walk from my house. We had gone to the hills in March which was end-of-crop harvest to pick up a wild fruit called mazhange. Sometimes, we were then lucky to have to encounter baboons in their environments. Toward the east was a vast flat land of red soil and houses weren't visible. Further down, the land loses its flatness to more gorgy, large trees, and roads become twist and twister and was more of a signal that you are about to join the main road to the city. Bigger hills appeared like a rule; they stretched along the main road and a few mountains begin to appear and gradually in the same manner but further away from the road. Some of these mountains had names, in my grandmother's never ending stories. The beauty of my village was it was sitting on the neck-spine angle of the valley. It kind of made it cozier. With the disadvantage being that most seasons we had to walk further out to the hills for wood and other necessities that were wild. Each side of the veiled provided seasonal eatables such as fruits, mushroom, and caterpillars.

As we did not have televisions in those days, evening entertainment was all about story telling. The greatest story teller of all was my oldest aunty Marita. Whenever she had come for special supper at our house, she will leave when every one of us had tears in our eyes from laughing. Most weekends I had stayed at my grandmother's house which she shared with Prisca. Prisca was the only child of my father's younger sister, and she was brought up by our grandmother. We were the two favorite grandchildren until when the older cousins came to visit from the city with all her treats. In her kitchen was the place where we would all sleep as this was the warmest part of the house. I believe my grandmother never had any fairy stories as every story she told us had a backing of proof. Around the fire my grandmother would tell us about how she would bully everyone because of her strength, beauty, and statue. She also talked about the wars and superstitious events that happened way before my father's time. My grandmother never told us about her personal life such as how she came to have three children fathered by three different men. She also never mentioned her children's difference and I now know why it was not important for her children to dwell on who was who. I knew a lot about who was who too, only my mother told us.

On the other hand when at my parents' house we had always sung and pray. The only time we read together with our mother was when we were reading the Bible which was every evening before bed. We had make turns to read the bible every night as my mother could not read. The funniest thing was she always demanded the verse she wanted read and also knew the topic, chapter, and page number. Sometimes she did find herself the joke of the night as we would laugh at this. I had thought my mother was a very intelligent woman and what she could have achieved if she was not an orphan. Fighting was not one thing she favored; she had a stammer and she always got the names mixed to whom she was angry with and sometimes she would laugh while phewming to the course; when one of us suddenly said, "I am not the person you are talking to," stopping her from being angry.

There was never a dull day inside my family home. During my youngest years of growing up, there were always up to seven children at a time. Dinnertime was always an occasion. My mother with the help of my older sister and nieces would cook a big feed. We had shared food in a traditional way, sitting around the circle using our half-washed hand sometimes dripping dirt water. It was always the case of you having to start at the beginning or you would miss out. Occasionally, my niece called Musafare, had to cry as she was the cry baby and my mother's favorite. She also took the advantage that her grandmother would always come to her rescuer and always end up sharing dinner with her and this was one of the reasons my mother never knew why she was always being picked up on. It gave the boys something to tease her about. What I enjoyed about growing up in my mother's house was the characters each of us presented and somehow my mother knew how to acknowledge them all. We never played with outsiders unless they were our cousins which were nearly everyone in the village.

One day I, my young brother Alfred, Naomi, my half-sister, David, my half-brother, Musafare, my niece, and Bondi, my nephew, of who were all younger than me, went for a walk as we usually did. My parents had over forty acres of land and the other end heading south had red sand. It was a lovely bright sunny afternoon which was normal around March. We walked through our vegetable garden which was at the rear section of our house. There was a water hole used for watering the vegetables during of rain seasons. We walked through some small bushes and find ourselves out in the red soil field. My mother grew peanuts every other year and sometimes round nuts. We had liked going there to pick up left over nuts like little monkeys would. There was only one small anthill in this stretch of the field. On the far side we could see the headmaster's house that was by the main road. This main road led to the the only hospital in the city then to Salsbury now Harare. As we proceed with our playful walk, I suddenly felt like someone was watching us. I stopped and looked back so as my little siblings. What we saw was what we have heard our elders talk about. We saw a family of short people made out of the red soil moving toward us. We ran as fast as our little legs could carry us. One thing I never forget about this day is; as children we never discussed our difference. We were brought up by one mother. In actual fact, when my second mother ran away, David was just eight months old. My mother had to breast-feed both boys as twins. As I was the fastest runner, I was leading the race; Alfred was second followed by Naomi then David. David suddenly called out, "Naou, please wait for your brother!" Naou was short for Naomi; that's how he had always called her. This sudden remembrance of who was who on this day did not come into my mind until we were much older, when we had used this phrase to tease David. Back to the little dwarves we had encountered, we were breathless by the time we got home. We could not talk and my mother wondered if we had seen a ghost during daylight. After we had managed to talk, as usual my mother managed to assure us that in summer there are small anthills that form which can look like a family. We thought that was the biggest lie she ever told us, but we were brought up to understand mothers are always right even if they are wrong.

The next day early in the morning, my mother made a visit to my grandmother's house. As usual I would take any opportunity to accompany her. While talking to my grandmother, I heard her say; "The children saw chidhokwana" short for short people. There was a little whisper kind of talk that appeared serious. Chidhokwana were people who were perceived as powerful and lived among humans and were invisible. To be able to see these people could cause harm and only spirited people were believed to have the powers to encounter them. At the end of the day, my grandmother came with some mixed herbs of leaves and bark, put it in large bucket of water, and we all had to wash our bodies in this medicated water. As usual I was always the one to initiate a gossip, so I told everyone why we had to wash with medicated water. I also made sure what I had told them was never to be repeated. My grandmother taught me a lot about superstitious happenings and that I had to remember that these events were to be respected.

Growing up the traditional way taught me that mothers were capable of administering multiple tasks without formal qualifications. Women were cooks, farmers, midwives teachers of every subject and that is how my family structure was. Most men worked in the cities and visited their family weekends. We had always helped our mother with fieldwork during rainy season. Most times was work before we attended school and Saturdays. Friday was a *spiritual* day of which my mother would attend women church group so they were never work to do except house work so as Sunday was church day. As I was the last in the family, I got to notice how much my mother was absent. Every year after harvesting she visited my father in the city for a break and would go for some weeks at end. Just before rainy season, she would also go for fertilizer and seed shopping for our household, grandmother's and untie Marita's. My sister Venencia looked after all of us during these times. Venencia was a couple of years older than me, and Charles was the brother between us followed by my little brother Alfred. The rest of the children were my nieces, nephews, one half-brother and sister. Although I had five older sisters, most of them had been married or moved out of home way before I was old enough. When it comes to boyfriends, my mother had a strict rule on this—no boys at all, especially if they were teens. This is because my sister Venencia liked boys as I saw it then. Because of this I was my mother's watchdog, especially those days when she takes vacations for some time out. As a result of my work I became my sister's worse enemy and we were never friends even when we were adults. Looking back I was a bad watchdog because some of the stories I was telling my mother were made up just to make sure she got the beating. The older I got the more apparent I became to my mother; she realized I was what she called—my grandmother's grandchild—and she disapproved most of my grandmother's behavior. Taking the advantage of my status I became quite rebellious when required to share duties, and this made my mother mad. One day she did lose her composure and told me the truth about my name. What she said was "I don't like that name of yours and as far as I am concerned that's not your name." I was only eight or nine years of age, but I am sure I was my grandmother's granddaughter. I asked my older sister Venencia what was all that about. That was a lucky day for Venencia who always got a hiding because of me and I needed help. As she was a couple of years older she knew about how I became Sophia, and she enjoyed telling me the story. It was a funeral in my heart to find out that the name that gives me so much authority was not my real name after all, so I paid my grandmother a visit. To get to my grandmother's house was a good fifteen minutes' walk. I cried and sobbed all the way, and she could hear me wailing crossing the bridge, past her sister's house to her frontyard. Before I could tell her what had happened; somehow she knew it had something to do with my mother. I only had to say, "She said Sophia was not my real name," and we were on our way across the bridge back to my house. Strange as it is, I found out at a very young age how much my mother's life, especially married life, depended on my grandmother. Somehow couple of years later, I could logically see my family life and the relationship within and stopped being the cause for fights between my mother and grandmother. Something about these issues I felt was never solved, and I found myself preferring to be addressed as Sophie rather than Sophia. That was only at school at home no one would dare disrespect my grandmother.

My house was by the schoolyard, and behind the school was the main road that had only two buses a day. One that goes to the city at eight in the morning and one that comes from the city reaching our village at four. Fridays only will have one more late bus at ten thirty that brought people from the city after work for the weekend. Below the school yard was the river and just across the bridge before the shopping center was my grandmothers' house this was the only shopping center that supplied dozens of villages. At the shopping center were three stores; the largest one was a general store. Outside the general store was a mill. In those days the weather seemed always hot than cooler and when it rained we could smell the rain an hour before it reaches our area. Rainy season was the scariest thing I could remember when I was young; the thunder would sound more like nuclear power lifting up the earth and the lightning, the most spectacular thing I had ever seen. When lightning in the dark, we could find a lost needle in the dirt. As spectacular as all this was, I learnt about lightning's danger because there was always a fire in the distance of a hut burning or sometimes a funeral the next day caused by it.

I attended the local school up to almost grade seven. My school years are memorable due to the fact that I was always on top of the class, especially in mathematics, geography and sports. I had played netball and ran short relays representing the school during provincial games. And always was the teacher's favorite, maybe because my family were friends of the longest and only headmaster I ever knew at our school. His name was Mr. Dangarembwa and his wife was the a head mistress.

School was one of the most enjoyable days of my childhood. We had general work school work, cutting grass, picking up rubbish, vegetable gadening and some of us were chosen to help in teachers houses. The teacher's houses were part of the school. I was always chosen to work at Mrs. Dangarebwa,s house. We had cleaned the house, preparing maize meal or make peanut butter the traditional way. All this was part of learning. On sports days the whole school participated with our parents coming to watch us. I began playing sport in third grade. I was lucky because the sport co-odinator was my father,s cousin's daugher, her name was Ms. Makuto. I was a sprinter in short rellays, hundred metres and I was a defender in netball for the school team.

One story I had not forgotten was when I had to be the first pupil to refuse to go to school. In those days noone could dare miss school because they wanted to all they disagree with an event. A boy called Insurance had an unusuall dislike to me. He had bullied me and pick on me basically making my days at school unpleasant. One day he took his bulling a lot further by accusing me of littering on the school yard. That was an offence, the biggest one I was just to commite was when he had gone to report me to the headmaster's. He had been send back to get me but pretended to do so. He went back to the headmaster and told him I refused. The headmaster then sent two prefects to carry me back to his office. I got my first coporal punishment. From the office I went to my granmother's house tears and snort everywhere. I told her I was never to go to school ever again, she promised to take care of things. She talked to my mother and kept me off school for few days. My mother told the headmaster why I was not at school and that my grandmother was allowing this behaviour. One morning the headmaster showed up at my granmother's house, after he had gone my granmother said I should go back to school she had sorted the matter and assured me Assurance was not to pick up on me again.

Even that was disrupted when war broke out in 1975. I was twelve years old by then. War has been going on for some time; only it had not reached our province. In one sunny quiet morning we were confronted by helicoptors in the air, lorries and tankers on ground like dogs gathering sheep. The Rhodesian army had a message for everyone on gun point. Without notice we were to pack our belongings and camp at the school grounds. At the school grounds we were told where our protected villages were going to be. Near the school ofcause and that was for every village to be at their nearest school. Over night we were living like squatters and curfew was imposed. We had kept going to school as my school was inside the protected village, but school was no fun anymore.

I was thirteen years by this time; one day something happened that changed my already changing life forever. I was walking from school. The village was quite as most adults would have gone back to check on stock and crops during the day. I was taken away by the army that was patrolling the village. After I was instructed to follow them to where their lorries were waiting, there I realized I was not the only one. They were few other teens, some even in school uniforms. After we were loaded in several army lorries, we were then driven to another village about an hour's drive. During school sport trips, I had traveled in this route we took this day and remembering seeing cows, goats and people walking mainly waving at the school lorry. To and from through these villages; were always the memories of going to play sports so we sing so loud that our opponents could hear us long before we get there. My school was the best in sports we rarely lost. I could hardly recognize anything; this place had become a ghost village without the village. I had not imagined how far war had traveled to reach my dear village and something immediately awakened. It was the awakening of the fear my parents had never taught me, the fear of humans. On our arrival at the place we were being taken to, I felt we were in for a nasty experience. We were ordered to sit under a huge Mahobahoba tree in silence. This tree had a trunk the size of a hut. It looked like people had lived around it for a million years, but they were nowhere to be seen. There were also many more lorries arriving carrying younger people.

The place had been turned into an army barrack with underground bunkers and watching towers in every angle. These bunkers had walls built out of sandbags. One by one we were called in for questioning inside the underground bankers. In the bunker were two white soldiers and one black one. I think his task was to translate. The big, fat, and bald soldier spoke to the black solder, as I could already speak English I heard what he said, then I realized that he was one of the most feared ones. I had overheard the villagers saying, "If you are caught by the South African soldiers, they don't have mercy." He had a very distinctive accent from that of the white Rhodesians I had met during school holiday when we had visited the city. I reply without waiting for the black soldier to translate. I didn't know of the terrorist as they were called, and I had never seen any villagers carrying food to the hills. He said if I did not tell the truth I will regret. The black soldier had instructed me to sit on the sand floor with legs stretched apart; my next answer was not completed as the bigger white soldier repeatedly whipped the inside of my thighs. Several of those were enough to cut my soft young skin open and blood splattered out of my legs and on to my dress. This was the first beating for a princess that I was. Not even my mother could lay a hand on me. I immediately remembered what she used to say, "If you keep crying, I will give you something to cry about." This experience was not one to cry about. No one was going to rescue me, not even my grandmother. Days later we were sent back home walking. It took us half a day to reach our village. It was a difficult walk as I had to walk like I had been raped by a thousand men. My inner thighs were raw. As for boys, most of them had bumps on their heads and their backs were dripping off flesh. Together we walked and walked as we entertained ourselves with what we would do if we had power on our side. During this trip back, I learnt from the other kids that these people the soldiers are looking for existed and they were more powerful than the white ones. I went home with the idea I would like to meet them.

It did not take long before the wounds healed. A few weeks later I met up with the other kids I had met at the army camp. They seemed to know how we could escape and join the freedom fighters. One day with no food or change of clothes we ran away from home toward Mozambique. After what appeared to be a few weeks of hiding by day and traveling by night, I was very skinny, my shoes had no sole, and my dress had lost its color. I was so skinny, any modeling agent would have liked to use me for a modern cat walk. Some of my friends had been killed or displaced during air raids. The night I finally met the freedom fighters I felt really blessed. It was the experience I had not even dreamt of. Chanting, dancing, and singing was all the freedom fighters did. Deep down all that brave look was a sacrifice I witnessed, so was their speech. "Some of you won't make it. Therefore it is OK to return home and find ways to help win the war." When I heard I may never see my mother again, and at this time this was no joke, I had witnessed the horrible death of some of my friends. I was not sure anymore if I wanted to pursue what I thought was the only way to save our village. And the freedom fighters had said this is no task for those who would look back. Many kids from the village were being taken on a daily basis. I am sure because of this my mother and grandmother thought that I had been taken by the soldiers again. A shower and a meal was all I wanted. When I had reached home my parents did not ask me a word of what happened; I think the state of me told the story. They cuddled me as I cried for my friends; I could not go and tell their families what had happened to them. I cried for all the things I grew up with that had vanished like wind. I cried for all the old people that had lost their dignity and replaced with the darkest sorrows. I cried for my village that had a new face of horror, and I cried when I looked at my body that was now covered with scars caused by other humans. This was the last time I called Murewa my home as the next morning I was sneaked away by bus to Salisbury accompanied by my mother.

Salisbury was the only safe place for younger people and villages were now only for those who could not escape or too old to run. I had always liked Salisbury; I used to come and visit my father or my older sisters during some school holidays. There was a big gap between myself and my sister Monica, the one I was to go and live with. Her own children were old enough to look after themselves except the youngest boy that went to live with his sister in the other part of the city to escape war. Monica was an acclaimed chef working in big hotels, and at this stage she was working for one of the richest Rhodesian migrants from Italy who owned the largest textiles of that time, probably in the world. My brother Charles, just a year older than me, had been offered a job at the textile factory. His boarding school had been burned down by the freedom fighters which had become a trend around the country. I lived with my sister till I was seventeen. During this period she had tried to get me work as a housekeeper and lasted no more than a week. The village was very protective of me. I never knew what it means to be black. As a child I grew up knowing that white people were sophisticated, intelligent, and superior. No one told me this, but it was obvious especially on one occasion when we were visiting my sister in the city. When we got off the bus, we had to walk through a white suburb and walk for some time before reaching our destination. My mother was carrying a bag on her head; my little brother Alfred on her back and on each side was my hand and my Brother Charles's hand. Two white kids aged seven and ten came rushing on their bikes and one of them hit the bag off my mother's head and it dropped to the ground. This was despite that my mother had made way on the footpath for them to pass. I remember her muttering all the way home; that's how upset she was. At this stage, I had all the information already from the failed trip to Mozambique about how the world needed to change. To my surprise I learnt that being black means dirty and anything below dirty. Somehow I could not behave the black way, so I got fired every time I got a job.

I had been living in the city for a year and the country was on fire. It was the time my father had a stroke. I can still see the pain he endured from losing his life at such a difficult time. We were lucky he pulled through that but could never work again. I blocked the horrors of wars that were getting worse by the day, petrol tanks being blown up, and news was all about who was dying and where the action was. I became a city girl; my sister was all I needed to teach me about life in the city. I had new clothes, shoes, even haircut. I learned to speak and walk like a woman. It wasn't long before I had my own friends to go to the movies with unlike in the village where we used to watch projected images that did not talk, once a year on the school building wall. Projected movies of how white people lived with black men at their mercy as servants. I got to go and watch live music of the bands I had only known through the radio. Life was so great yet beneath it all I knew what my village was going through and that I will never go back home again. Years had gone by and the war was getting worse so as the life in the city. The cities had become overcrowded and this caused crime, poverty, and everything that gets created from wars.

I finally got a real job after three years of living off my sister who did not mind at all. The CID boss was my aunt's boyfriend and this connection helped me to get a job as a personal secretary for Mr. Gallagher, a senior army sergeant. I got to know quite a few policemen and army corporals. I was much independent from my sister by now and seventeen. I was even surprised that I was still a virgin when all girls would have babies by fifteen years of age. Having a child too many saved them from having to be taken by soldiers for cooking, cleaning, and sex.

Stupidity is one of those things girls do when they find out their ratings are higher than the girl next door. Life was on its peak; danger was now more fun than anything else. I was being counted for by my parents as a life saver as I could afford to contribute money for their everyday needs apart from what my other sisters and brother were already doing. I got pregnant by a policeman that I met at my auntie's house. I had thought he was my boyfriend and that's all I needed to know at that time. On finding out that he was already someone's husband, I did not know how I was going to tell my parents, especially my sister that loved me and trusted me with all her heart. Worried about my family if they should find out, I moved out of home and went flatting with my friend Gladys. I hid the pregnancy for ten months. I did not even know I was way overdue as I did not visit a doctor. As a result of this I had a still birth. Life went back to normal, but not long after this I met someone who was the love of my life. Again the absence of streetwise caused me to have a baby boy before marriage. This time it was OK. I could take care of the baby and myself. Also my parents had not shown disappointment when I had told them of the baby on the way. All the love I had for the father of my baby I transferred it to his son. I was in love with my son from the first day he kicked my belly. The country was on fire and rumors of independence proved to be true. And that was good news for the country as for individuals it was time to figure out how they could go back to their original life. As for me it was also time to figure out how I was going to live for the future in a new country.

With the coming of independence so was the opening of the whole wide world experience. During war we had been promised live the way white people lived and have access to a better life. How this was going to happen I had no idea, but I was not the only one. I had the best life coach in life and that was my oldest sister Monica. She had always taught me that life does not come to you unless you go looking for it. I was always moving with time, and you could only find me where there was action. The visibility for change was obvious, and there was one law for all.

The once Rhodesian colony was now the Republic of Zimbabwe, and if you could not capitalize just on the change of name, you could by changing countries. And that's what a lot of white people did so also the new expatriates coming to Zimbabwe. Lucky me that is when I met my husband who had come to experience 'the help out build Zimbabwe" as an expatriate. He had come from England to teach physics and mathematics. A year later, we had a baby girl. While looking after kids, I took up a secretarial course in the capital city of Harare that used to be called Salisbury. I also worked for foreign researchers that were conducting research on Zimbabwe's traditional medicines. This was probably the happiest time in my life. I had made it through the war, not even one of my family members lost life during war, and now I had two children and another on the way. My husband had spoken of going to live overseas, and he had stressed it was a good idea for the kids. With all the information he had told me about living in London, I thought it will be better if I had one more child before traveling. Life in Zimbabwe was easy for me in every way. I had a home in a previously whites-only suburb. I had a housekeeper and a gardener to make life easy. No wonder every black person wanted to live in an equal society.

Overwhelmed by the changes and starting to grow as a person I could see the opportunities ahead. Having been accustomed to suffering and death, I did not know the worst of the worst was sitting on my doorstep. As I was expecting I had a baby girl. At three months I lost her to cot death, I had never ever heard of cot death, but this is what happened according to the coroner's report. For the months that followed I wish I could understand for that took all whom I was to a new level of pain. I almost lost my mind grieving and when dealing with what grief is that is one thing I know very well. After loosing my baby my plans to move overseas became more urgent as. My husband got a job in New Zealand and we left Zimbabwe. I was happy for many reasons and sad for a few.

Where I was going, how far, how long and what I was going to learn is today another subject. I never thought about that aspect of life or life as an aspect. What I know is the the time I left my homeland I was not scared to leave. I had left my village way too young to start a life in a city and even then I never knew what I was going to do next. What I believe now is that I was part of the nature and whatever it was deciding to do was the direction I was going to end up in, just like a leaf in a very large river. I believe if what I know now is what I am able to live by and constract this inorder to offer this being to the world, I will be the happiest woman who ever lived. At the age of thirteen, I had not even thought about what I was going to do. I was a kid at school, and all of a sudden, I congratulated myself for having been at an unacknowledged university. If I had known way back then that I would ask questions about my existence, after I have already existed, I would not have been lost.

I miss you

The river that floods whenever it rains
The danger that lies on the steep side
The steep side that flood before it rains
For thou I miss you
Friday, Friday my holy day
The offering to the sprit
For thou they could see us
For thou they could nature us
For thou I miss you

Friday for the men and their cows
The cows that had their day
A day to dip off the infections
The dung and the smells
The whistles and moo moos
For thou I miss you

Children of the lands
Playing in the dusty fields
Fields filled with locusts and bugs
For the catch will take home
Locusts and bugs the offering of the day
For that was enough for the child of the land
For thou I miss you

After that many years
Are you there are you there
After that many years can you hear me
After that many years can you hear me
For thou I miss you

O Super force
O Super Force
Can you hear me
Can you hear me
For thou I miss you

I can not

I cannot help another person when I cannot help myself.

I cannot love another person when I don't know the meaning of love.

I cannot respect sex when it has no meaning in life.

I cannot be part of the sea when my stream brings pollution.

I cannot accept a second chance without a purpose for it.

I am what I am today, because of what I learn yesterday.

I cannot bring my children back, but shall cherish them.

I cannot mend the broken hearts I caused, except to reach out for them.

I cannot part with the virus I live with, so I will accommodate it till death.

I cannot change what I taught my children nor shall deny that their lives have been a result of the environment I provided.

I shall remain humbled to my kids for what they have become. Therefore, I am open to sharing and helping today and tomorrow's generations my commitment.

Not the End Yet

To participate on Sophie's cause Visit:
www.sophiesworldthejourneys.com

CONTRIBUTIONS

Front Photo by: Joseph Djugum at www.sophiesworldthejourneys.com

Author photographed by: lynn at www.lynnclaytonphotography.com

Author stylist: Rohini Jay at Brand-me@hotmail.com

ABOUT THE AUTHOR

Sophie was born in 1963 in Rhodesia in the province of Murewa. During her teens, Sophie witnessed the suffering of her people caused by war and then moved to New Zealand at the end of the war when Rhodesia became Zimbabwe. Sophie became one of the very first black women to settle in New Zealand. Unfortunately, her new found world turned grey, and forgot who she was. For twenty-four years she lived like someone else. Through a miracle she came back to remember who she was. Today Sophie strives to tell stories about survival, miracles, self healing and the beauty of understanding the purpose of life. Her passion is about what she discovered in her strangle and she now lives to honor that process. Now a grandmother with life filled with joy and a promising future, Sophie awaits for her next journeys. Her first publication and activities now available.

You can contact Sophie at . . . . www.sophiesworldthejourneys.com